I0528169

Stages

My Life in Stories

Stages

My Life in Stories

Jessica Piscitelli Robinson

TUCKER
DS
PRESS

Stages: My Life in Stories ©2024 Jessica Piscitelli Robinson

All Rights Reserved.
Reproduction in whole or in part without the authors' permission is strictly forbidden. All photos and/or copyrighted material appearing in this publication remains the work of its owners. This book is not affiliated with any studio or production company. This is a scholarly work of review and commentary only, and no attempt is made or should be inferred to infringe upon the copyrights of any corporation.

Cover design by Bart Robinson
Author Photo by Robert Merhaut
Edited by David Bushman
Book designed by Scott Ryan

Published in the USA by Tucker DS Press
Columbus, Ohio

Contact Information
Email: TuckerDSPress@gmail.com
Website: TuckerDSPress.com
Twitter: @FMPBooks
Instagram: @Fayettevillemafiapress
ISBN: 9781959748120
eBook ISBN: 9781959748137

To my loves. I love you more.
-Me

CONTENTS

Chapter 1

Daddy's Car

In August of 2006 my dad called to tell me that the doctors found a lump the size of a grapefruit in his lungs. Small-cell lung cancer. The doctors gave him a year to live, but just a few years earlier my mom had been given the same prognosis, and she'd survived only three months.

I was raised by my mom. She was a fantastic mom, and it killed me when she died. When I got off the phone with my dad, there was no question in my mind—I knew he was going to die. What I told myself, in that moment, was "At least it won't be as devastating as when mom died."

My parents divorced when I was four. The only memories I have from before the divorce are of screaming and crying—my dad screaming and me crying. He wasn't a bad man, it was just a bad marriage, and I was the last of three kids who all added stress to an unhappy situation.

After he moved out, I got to see my dad only on weekends, not even every weekend. He was my dad, and he was gone. He became the thing I wanted most in the world. My life became a waiting game.

The weekends when he'd call to say he was coming, I sat in the front window and watched for him. It felt like forever. As each car approached the house, I repeated over and over, with building excitement, "Daddy's car, Daddy's car, Daddy's car." And then, as the car inevitably passed by, I sighed, "Not Daddy."

He was always late. I was heartbroken because he never showed up when he said he would. When my dad arrived, he'd find me in tears. Mom would calm me down, get me quiet, and dad would apologize to me. I forgave him. He was my dad and he was finally there. While he'd cook and laugh with whatever adult he'd brought with him—his girlfriend or siblings—he'd send me away to watch TV. Though I wasn't allowed to hang out with the adults, I felt good knowing my dad was there. Until he left again, seemingly right after he'd arrived.

After what seemed like years of hoping he'd get there sooner and stay longer, reality sank in—he wasn't going to arrive on time. He wasn't going to spend the time with me, talk to me the way he talked to the adults who always surrounded him on his visits, be there for me. And so, I stopped waiting.

By the time I became a teenager, weekly visits turned into monthly visits and then sometimes not even that. Dad didn't yell very often anymore. I knew how to avoid angering him. I kept quiet and followed orders. I accepted his rule, but I lost that hero worship. I started to see him as a man.

He was bad-tempered. He drank too much. He'd made a lot of mistakes in his life, and sometimes acted as if his kids were some of them. He made me feel like a responsibility—someone who required too much of his time and money—not like the most important person in the world.

Still, I didn't want to give up on him. He was my dad. He deserved a chance to prove he loved me. So, I played a kind of game. I stopped calling him. Weeks went by before he finally called me. When he did, he gave me a guilt trip. "What's going on? You can't call your father anymore?"

I said, "I could say the same to you, Dad. You didn't miss me?"

He didn't hesitate. "I was waiting for you to call me. If you want to talk to your father, you should call him."

I did want to talk to him, but what I wanted more was for him to want to talk to me. So, I went back to waiting for him to call, to testing him, and that's when we really grew apart, because he failed.

Over the years, I finished college, started my career, and moved to Virginia. I called my dad, periodically. I saw him, rarely. We lived our own lives, separated by space and the kind of distance that builds up over a lifetime. Then he got a chest cold, in the middle of summer.

When my dad found out he was dying, he changed. Facing his own mortality, he came alive. He fought hard to live. He made it past a year, and then another and then two more. He went to treatment and therapy and the pharmacy like it was his job, and he'd always been good at his job.

Once he had the treatment plan down, my dad started working on his personal life. He began to talk to me, like he'd never been able to before.

Dad gave me a different perspective on my childhood—through his eyes. He opened up about how he changed when my older brother turned two, and turned challenging. My dad hadn't wanted to become his own father—yelling, screaming, and hitting at the slightest provocation—but toddlers don't know how to show respect, and my dad demanded nothing less. He hadn't wanted to be apart from us, but he worked two hours away from our home. When my mom kicked him out, it made sense for him to live closer to his work than to his kids.

My dad never really offered me advice. Perhaps he didn't think he could. He did start asking me questions about my life. How was my job? Everything in the house working? What about the boy I was dating? It felt like he actually wanted to get to know me, like he cared about who I was. Most important to me, he no longer waited for me to call him. He called every day if he hadn't heard from me first.

I started playing a new game with him. At the end of every phone call, he'd say "goodbye," and then I'd say "goodbye" and hang up. As I was hanging up, though, I'd hear him say "I love you." Then, of course, I needed him to know that I'd heard him, so I'd call him back and say "I love you too." Then we'd laugh and hang up again. And so, I started waiting, at the end of every call, for him to say "I love you" before hanging up, and he never let me down.

As his cancer got worse, he and I grew closer. I drove to see him just about every weekend. Whenever I called to tell him I was getting on the road, he'd ask if I was crossing the Delaware—the halfway point on my drive to his house. "No, Dad, just getting in the car now." It was never soon enough for him. He was waiting for me, and I was always late. I'd spend the weekend, sometimes longer, and we had a great time, just hanging out.

Leaving was the hard part. He seemed to "forget" when I was going to leave. If it was Sunday and I was packing, he'd say, "I thought you were staying until Monday." If it was lunch time he'd say, "I'm making a sauce for dinner. What kind of pasta do you want?"

When I'd get in the car to go, he'd come out on the front porch to watch me drive away. He'd stand there and wave until I couldn't see him in my rearview mirror anymore. It made me cry, every time—not only because I felt so bad leaving him, but also because I knew how hard it was to watch someone you love drive away.

On the weekends my father visited me as a little girl, I stood at the front door and waved as Daddy got in his car. Something broke in me each time he pulled out of the driveway, and as he started down the road, I ran outside and chased after him, feet pounding on the sidewalk, arms waving, yelling "bye Daddy, bye Daddy" until I couldn't keep up and his car grew small with distance.

When I used to think about how I'd chase Daddy's car, I felt so angry that my father could just drive away. Now, all I can think is how hard it must have been for him each time, as hard as it was for me all those years later. My dad may not have beaten cancer, but he found a way to heal both of us.

Chapter 2

Scraped Knee

As a working mom, I struggle with trying to live up to the childhood my stay-at-home mom gave me. My kids have been in daycare since they were a few months old. I didn't leave the nest until kindergarten. My kids wear store-bought Halloween costumes, whereas my mom always made ours from scratch—and they were amazing. My birthday parties were in our backyard, with activities planned and carried out by my mom, who also made the cake or cupcakes. My kids' birthdays are at places that host parties and provide all the food other than the cake, which I buy. My mom knew all our teachers' names and spent hours volunteering at the schools. I struggle to sign all the papers my kids bring home and return to the school on time.

I try to give my kids as much as my mom gave me, but in most ways, I just can't. More than anything, I want to spend more time with my kids, and I want them to know that I love spending time with them. My mom was so involved in my life, but she sometimes made me feel like she wanted anything other than to spend one more minute with me.

Mom didn't have to work until I got to sixth grade, so we had her all to ourselves. Before my mom started work, she was a full-time mom to me and my older brother and sister. And that kept her very busy. In addition to cleaning the house, buying groceries and clothes and supplies for all of us, and maintaining the house, she volunteered at the school and soccer games and Scouts, drove us around, hosted playdates, made our costumes, and provided emotional support to us as well as to many of our friends. She was a loving, caring mom who told me she loved me every day. But she was also an eighties mom.

In the eighties, we didn't have helicopter parenting so much as rocket launcher parenting. Parents would raise their kids until they were able to feed themselves, go potty by themselves, and, most importantly, turn the TV on by themselves, and then they were done with having to parent. Eighties parents, in my experience, wanted kids to be seen and not heard, didn't give praise freely, certainly never gave medals (unless a kid actually won at something), and wouldn't pay for a doctor unless the kid was dying. As my mom would put it, "Don't bother me unless you're bleeding to death."

As a single mom, she got no help from my dad. I was the youngest—a surprise baby who came along after my parents' marriage was already mostly over—and I think by the time I was eight, my mom was just tired of being a supermom. She'd had more than her fair share of kid time, and by that summer, she was done. Summer was always the worst for Mom—us kids hanging around the house all day—because the internet, and its ability to absorb a mind for hours on end, hadn't been invented yet. At some point, Mom started kicking us out of the house in the morning, telling us not to come back until the streetlights came on. She did not want us to bother her unless we were bleeding to death.

I was the baby, and so sometimes it took me a little bit longer to get out the door. My mom would start nudging me, saying,

"Go. Get out there."

By the time I'd be ready to leave the safety of my home, my brother and sister were long gone, off doing whatever. I was left to my own devices. And, of course, that meant I wanted to stay with Mom, play with her. I'd say, "There's nothing to do. What should I do?"

She'd respond, "Go play in the street."

I think she was kidding. Yeah, I'm sure she was kidding.

The summer I was eight, my dad brought us a puppy. A little yellow mutt that grew up to look exactly like a dingo. I wanted to name the dog Scooter because that seemed like a good name for a dog, but my brother—he was older and he won the argument—named the dog after his favorite character on his favorite TV show, the very classy classic *Dukes of Hazzard*. Scooter became Cooter, and Cooter became my best friend.

I started taking Cooter with me everywhere I went, whether or not she liked it. This one summer day, I took Cooter to my favorite place, Indian Hill, the nearby park named after the Indian corn that grew on the hill. Cooter and I headed to my favorite part of Indian Hill, which was, of course, the tire park.

The tire park was a playground made out of tractor tires bolted together to form swings and jungle gyms and steps and obstacles. As was our way in the eighties, it wasn't as safe as you might think a park made from rubber would be. I took Cooter with me on the tire swing, which was just a giant rubber tire with big metal bolts sticking out at weird angles, hanging from a fat, not-covered-in-anything-to-make-it-safer chain. Cooter was okay on the swing. It didn't swing very much due to its size and shape compared with my own lack of heft.

Then we went on another staple of any good eighties playground—the metal slide. The solid, 250-degrees-in-the-sun, never-gets-taken-away-until-it-rusts-clear-through slide. I went down a few times myself, and then I thought, *Well let me put the dog on it because you know she's gonna love it.* Cooter had little, sharp puppy-dog nails, but even those nails could not find purchase on that metal slide. She went down fast and flew right off the end, which she didn't like. I was not a terrible person, merely a lonely eight-year-old, so I only made her go down forty or fifty more times.

After the slide was exhausted, I took Cooter to my favorite part of the tire park—the jungle gym. The jungle gym consisted of big tractor tires bolted together in a cube, with a second cube on top of the first, like a tower of rubber tire cubes. There were eight towers connected together by bridges and tire steps.

I climbed all the way to the top of one of the tire towers, and of course I brought Cooter with me. I couldn't leave her down there in the lava. But Cooter didn't seem to like the view from the top that much. She was shaking and nervous. I put her on my lap to calm her down, but she wouldn't stop squirming around. She wouldn't sit still. And she started to slide.

The good news is that this time, her nails found purchase. The bad news is that it was in my leg. The skin on my leg stopped her from falling, for a second, before my skin broke. As she slid off, so did the skin on my thigh and knee.

She did not land on her feet, but she was fine. She stood there staring up at me with a look that said, *Maybe now you'll leave me alone?*

I didn't move, at first. I looked at my leg, and nothing was happening. It was great. I figured I got away unscathed. I didn't yet realize that when you get scratches with a razor blade, nothing seems to happen right away. And then it did. The blood, like the lava on the ground below, started to bubble up from underneath my skin, and then it started to pour out of the various cuts.

I was the baby of the family. By all accounts, and my own estimation, I was a big baby. But, for some reason, I did not start crying. Maybe I was in shock. Maybe some survival instinct I didn't know I had kicked in. I calmly climbed down from the tower. I got Cooter back on the leash, and we headed home.

I knew I was gonna need medical attention. We walked through the Indian cornfield, and over the dusty hill, and through the pine tree branches, and down the block to my house. When I got there, I let Cooter off the leash, and she ran and hid, never to be seen again. Then I called out for my mom, but she didn't answer.

I wasn't surprised that she wasn't there. It was the middle of the day in the summer, so Mom was where she always was—at her best friend, Carol's, house. This was before cell phones, so I knew Carol's phone number by memory. I walked over to the yellow rotary phone, attached to the kitchen wall, and dialed.

When Carol picked up, I said, "Hey, is my mom there?"

Carol was a mother herself. She was an eighties mom. She knew her duty was to protect my mom from her spawn. Carol said, "No. She's not here." And she hung up the phone.

I knew Carol well enough to know that if I called her back, she would not pick up. So the only thing I could do was to go to Carol's house, which, fortunately, was only another half block away.

By now, I was definitely feeling the pain. I limped across the street and up the block and knocked on Carol's screen door. I could see her sitting at her kitchen table. She very slowly got up—like she was really annoyed by my intrusion and wanted to be sure I knew—and walked slowly over to the door. When she opened the screen door, you might imagine a dramatic reaction, but she barely flinched at the sight of me.

I had on my Daisy Dukes, the bottom part of which was drenched, as if they had a maroon fringe. My leg was covered in blood, as were my knee-high tennis socks. My tennis shoes were pooling with blood, and I was just barely standing there, all lopsided. Carol took in the sight of me and called over her shoulder, "Your kid's bleeding."

My mom got up from the kitchen table, where she'd been sitting out of sight, came over to the door, and saw me. She didn't get mad at me for interrupting her Carol time. I looked enough like I was, indeed, going to bleed to death.

I was relieved she wasn't mad and relieved that I now had my mom. I figured she would take me to the hospital. Or the doctor. Mom was gonna take care of me. As she always did. She was exhausted from all the taking care of me that she had to do all the time, but she was a loving mom and a hugging mom and a taking-care-of mom. I was glad to be in her care again. I just didn't take into account—'cause in the moment how would I?—that she was also an eighties mom.

Mom walked me home. She didn't take me right to the car. She took me to the kitchen and had me climb up on the counter next to the sink. She took my socks and my shoes off, and then she had me put my leg over the kitchen sink. Then she did what any good mom of the eighties would do. She took out that giant brown, forty-gallon bottle of peroxide and just glug, glug, glugged all over my cuts. As I watched, the pieces of tire and Indian corn and puppy-dog nails bubbled out of me.

The scratches on my thigh looked red and swollen, but the one over my knee was clean as bone. I mean, it was clean down to the bone. When I saw my own kneecap, exposed, that is when I started freaking out. The shock wore off, and I started hyperventilating and crying and screaming. That didn't deter my mom. She took the skin that was hanging and she pushed it back into place, approximating where it was supposed to be. Then she wrapped some bandages around it and scooped me up in her arms. I thought, *Now, we're gonna go to the doctor*. But she didn't carry me to the car. She carried me to the couch, where she left me for the next several days.

She wasn't a complete monster. She turned on the TV. And she stayed with me in the house, taking her dates with Carol on the phone. Over the next few days, every time I had to move, any of the healing that had begun in my knee was undone. On the fourth or fifth day, when I got up to go to the bathroom, I limped past my mom, who was sitting at the dining room table smoking a cigarette. When she saw me with the blood newly dripping down my leg, again, she said, "We probably should have taken you to the doctor for stitches. Too late now."

I was eight, so I just said, "Yeah, I guess so." As I've grown up, a bit, since then, and as a parent of some pretty active kids myself, I'm now thinking, *No. If your leg is bleeding after several days, it is definitely not too late to go to the doctor.* But times have changed since I was the kid. Parenting has changed.

My mom was a super eighties mom. I had as much TV and as many TV dinners as I wanted while I recovered on the couch. I didn't get an infection, or lose the leg, or bleed to death. The wound eventually closed on its own, and Mom threw me out of the house again for the rest of that summer.

As a working mom, I don't have time to make costumes and host playdates and volunteer at the school. In those ways, I can't ever measure up to my mom. But I comfort myself by thinking that there's at least one way I can manage to parent better. At least, I hope so. All I need to do is avoid scarring my kids for life.

Chapter 3

The Biggest Loser

When I was ten years old, my life changed course and set me on a path to becoming a different person. I was in fifth grade. I was cute. I had big brown eyes, with thick, long eyelashes. I had crooked teeth, though I didn't yet care, and was always smiling. I wasn't popular but I wasn't unpopular either. I had my best friend, Joy, in my class. I had a couple other friends from the neighborhood. I was fine. It was good. I was happy.

Then, in the middle of fifth grade, Joey from Bayonne moved to town. In South Jersey, where I'm from, people don't talk like they're from Bayonne. Joey was new and cute and had a funny accent and all the girls in class wanted him. But I was cute too, so I got him.

In fifth grade, being boyfriend and girlfriend meant that when the bus would drop us off—we got off at the same bus stop— sometimes we'd go up on the hill and toss the ball. That's not a metaphor. We'd play catch. Sometimes we'd ride the seesaw. Also not a metaphor.

Things were going fine for a few weeks, and then this girl,

Rebecca, who was in our class, started teasing me. I hadn't been friends with her, but we weren't enemies or anything. Seemingly out of nowhere, she started picking on me. It was little things, like when I was giving a presentation, she'd make a little comment under her breath and everyone near her would laugh. Or in the lunchroom, she'd kind of bump into me and knock over my milk.

It wasn't awful, but I was upset. I told my mom about it. I was kind of angry with Rebecca and wanted to do something to her. I didn't have a plan; I just wanted revenge. My mom said, "Don't do anything mean. If you return meanness with meanness, it brings you down. It makes you low."

So, I tried to let it roll off of me, to not worry about it. After all, her behavior wasn't awful. It was just little rocks thrown, but it started an avalanche.

Joey, sensing that I wasn't the popular girl he'd assumed I was, broke up with me. That was fine. I was in fifth grade and didn't need a boyfriend. And the teasing kind of subsided. Rebecca seemed happy to leave me alone, and I thought it was over. That little bit of picking at me had passed. But those little things stuck. And worse, they stuck a target on my back.

Going into sixth grade, I was now unpopular, as in the opposite of popular. The popular kids were led by Jennifer. Then there were the kids in the middle, and then there were the losers. Being the most recent addition to the losers' club, I was kind of the queen of the losers. Either because they appointed me that or maybe because I just hadn't learned or realized my place yet.

I still thought I had the same rights as everyone else, still thought we were all equals. I took it upon myself to defend the other losers. There was the girl who got made fun of for being too fat and a boy who got made fun of for being too dumb and more than a few who got teased for being too smart.

And then there was Joy, again. My best friend was in sixth grade with me. She got made fun of for being poor. I was poor too. Or, at least, I wasn't a rich kid, like Jennifer. I got teased for being poor and being smart and most of all because Jennifer didn't like me. But for the most part, I was okay. Joy, not so much. Joy would come to my house on the weekends and she'd cry about how mean people were, and I told her what my mom told me. I told her, "It doesn't matter what other people think about you. The only thing that matters is what you think about yourself."

I don't think I understood the meaning of those words, not fully, but they sounded good when my mom said it to me, and I hoped they would help Joy. But they didn't. Or I assume they didn't based on what happened next. Shortly after spring break, Jennifer decided to take me down another notch. She took Joy away from me.

I don't know what happened, but one day Joy was my best friend and I was defending her from Jennifer, and the next day Joy was in with the popular girls and Jennifer started telling everyone that I thought I was better than them. She told everyone that I said I don't care what anyone thinks about me, that I was a snob, a princess. Everyone started calling me Princess, and the nickname stuck. As much as it hurt to be made fun of by Jennifer and the other kids, what hurt more was Joy. Joy leaving me, and betraying me. I felt like I couldn't trust anyone anymore.

But seventh grade. New year. New school. It was gonna be different. Better. It was a completely new group of people, and I thought we could start over. Only I didn't get into alpha track. Alpha was the smart kids' program and I was smart, but I wasn't quite smart enough. So I was put in with the general population. And I don't know if it was that they smelled the smart on me or maybe they saw the cracks that had started in fifth grade, but from day one, I was the biggest loser, with a huge target on my back.

Joe—different Joe—sat behind me in history class. He was about six feet tall, and he could reach my chair with his foot, so he would just kick me in the kidneys every day. It wasn't particularly painful, not physically, anyway, but it was annoying. In English class, this kid Craig sat behind me. He would spit in my hair. Sometimes he'd put gum in it. Then there were the twins, Jim and the other one, whose name I don't remember, so I'm gonna call him Tim. Jim and Tim had their lockers right next to mine. They were small, but together, they could shove me into the locker, and I gotta say, it's not as much fun as it looks in the movies.

I did have one friend in seventh grade. Maria. Another recent transplant from North Jersey. Maria was new and cute and shiny, and everyone loved Maria. But on the weekends, I got her. She was my best friend, at home. We would hang out at my house or hers, which was just up the street. We had so much fun together. I liked her parents. She liked my mom. We were close.

But in school, she was popular and I was not. Not only did she not defend me when I got teased, but she made fun of me too. She made stuff up about me. She'd say that I was so poor that we raised chickens in the yard to eat. She'd say that my dad was an alcoholic who was never around. The thing is, she was telling the other kids her own secrets, only saying they were mine. I knew this, but I would never reveal that about her. I wouldn't do that to a friend.

Every day of seventh grade, I went home and I cried. Sometimes, I didn't even make it through the day. I had to get sent home by the nurse because I was crying or having anxiety attacks. I'd cry to my mom, "Why? Why are people so mean?"

My mom didn't have an answer. I never did figure it out.

By the end of seventh grade, I couldn't take it anymore. On the last day of school, when Jim and Tim were coming toward me in the hallway, I lost my temper. I was near my locker, crying, and seeing them coming toward me, I just knew they were going to tease me. Why wouldn't they? So when they got close, I took Jim and I shoved him hard into the locker. He started crying.

Then I took Tim and I shoved him too. He didn't cry. He just got this look of shock on his face, as if he really hadn't known how much it hurt. I didn't feel good about hurting them. Well, okay, I felt a little bit good. But it wasn't like I completely changed, like I became someone who hurt others to make themselves feel better. And I knew that's what I had done. I didn't know how to go forward. I didn't know who to be. But I knew I wasn't that person.

That summer, when Maria came knocking, trying to be my best friend now that there was no one to see us, I didn't answer the door. I was done with her. I was done with all of it.

In eighth grade, I didn't try to make friends. I didn't try to defend anyone. I just tried not to be noticed. I kept my head down, never answered questions in class, sat alone at lunch, and got out of gym class as much as possible. It worked. I got through that whole year without being bullied, and without making a single friend. As much as seventh grade stands out as one of the worst years of my life, eighth grade stands out as the loneliest. And as painful as seventh grade was, I think eighth grade broke me.

Heading into high school, I was a different person from that cute and smiling fifth grader. The previous three and a half years had changed my outlook, my understanding of friendship, and me. I had internalized some lessons about trust, and love, and self-worth, that it would take me many more years to unlearn.

If I could go back to that girl about to once again start out at a new school with hopes of change that won't come yet, I would tell her, "It *does* matter what other people think about you, even though it shouldn't. It's too easy to listen to people who make you feel small. There will be many of them, but what they think shouldn't matter. What you think of yourself should be the most important thing. It's so easy to think yourself not worth loving. Know that you are deserving of love. Know that one day you will meet people who want to build you up, who will love you for being the creative, weird, and wonderful person that you are and that you will have a life surrounded by people you love, and who love you back."

Chapter 4

It's Complicated

The summer I turned twelve, my mom got diagnosed with breast cancer. My Babci, my grandma, came to stay with us—me, my mom, and my two siblings—for a week or two.

My mom and her mom, my Babci, had a complicated relationship. My dad always said that Babci had bile for blood. He thought Babci didn't like him because he was Italian. That may have had something to do with it, but I suspect his behavior was a bigger reason.

Babci and Grandpa, everyone called him Doc, didn't go to Mom and Dad's wedding. I wasn't there either. It was my older brother in Mom's belly. When they kicked Mom out of the house, she stayed with my dad's family until the wedding, and then my dad and mom got an apartment together.

After my brother was born, things between my mom and her parents started to mend. Or so I heard. It's complicated. She spent a lot of her time at Babci and Doc's house, with the baby. Doc came to love his grandkids. He never came to love my father, who was strict with us kids, sometimes inappropriately rough. When I, the youngest, was four years old, my Grandpa Doc died. I don't really remember him, but the stories I heard led me to understand that he was the warm parent, the loving parent, at least with my mom. She lost the parent she had felt closest to when he died.

I wasn't at the funeral, but Mom and her sister both told me the same story. They told me how Babci, who had just lost her husband, shushed them—her kids—and told them to stop crying. At their dad's funeral. "Stop that. Stop crying," she hissed.

Babci was of a different generation. She was a first-generation American. She was a woman of a different time. In Babci's time, American society cared more about a woman's appearance and conduct than her other qualities, and in Babci's time, society was important. There are lots of reasons why she might not have thought crying in public—even at your dad's funeral—was okay. Mostly, I think it came down to the fact that my mom and aunt were women, and women were meant to always look, and act, respectable.

It's complicated though. As a little girl, I was close to Babci. Sometimes Mom dropped me off at her house for the weekend, or a night. We'd stay up late watching Johnny Carson. She'd smoke, and I'd eat ice cream and practice twirling my hair the same way she twirled hers. She taught me to dance the Charleston. My mom and my brother and sister and I would spend at least a week at Babci's beach house every summer. Every day of our visit, Babci made us tuna fish sandwiches and bought us ice cream sundaes. She didn't eat much. She told my mom not to eat too much.

Babci told my mom that she'd never get or keep a man with all that weight on her, with those ankles. She worried that my older sister was already a "big" girl, and she didn't mean grown-up. She treated her sons like they could do no wrong and her daughters like they could do no right. And when my mom had a stroke and started to look and talk and move funny, not in a respectable way, Babci and her sons faded from our lives, as if Mom's "condition" were contagious, as if mom's slurred speech and cane would reflect poorly on them. When we were left impoverished on Mom's meager disability pay, it was too embarrassing to discuss, let alone address and assist. Money was not something respectable people talked about.

Mom had plenty of reasons to complain about Babci, but it's complicated. When Babci got older, ill, too old and ill to get out of bed, my mom, who was too poor most months to afford groceries, paid for a ride—if none of us kids were around to drive her - every day to and from the hospital to visit. My mom lay beside her mom on her last days and told her all the things you say to someone you love when they are dying. She's the one who stroked Babci's hair and told her she was going to be reunited with Doc and that it was okay to let go.

Mom loved her mom, my Babci. But the love between a mother and daughter is complicated.

I only ever saw Babci cry once. I don't know if my mom had seen her cry more than that one time. I never thought to ask her. It's possible it was the only time Babci ever cried in front of another person.

They didn't know I was watching. The advantage of being the youngest of three—I was often invisible, even at twelve, and especially on the day my mom came home from the hospital after her mastectomy. Babci helped Mom lay down on the couch.

I watched from the other room. The lights were dim. The house was quiet. Babci tucked my mom in. Mom said something to her. I couldn't hear. Maybe it was a thank you. Maybe it was I'm scared. Or don't leave. Maybe it was I love you.

Whatever my mom said, Babci held her hand and started to cry. It was only a second before she turned her face away, so my mom wouldn't see her tears. She held her daughter's hand and cried into the dark. It was complicated, but she was a mom who loved her daughter.

Chapter 5

High School Mosh Pit

High school was a mosh pit. Years bumping into years, bumping into expectations, disappointments, friendships made, friendships broken, boys, kisses, groping, crying, hiding, fighting, fleeing, sighing, finding, grinding, anger and release, and Lollapalooza.

Freshman year.

Trying to find myself, my voice, fit in, stand out, get by.

My face covered in acne. My teeth coated in braces. I couldn't talk to anyone or smile without covering my mouth. Kept my head down.

Left alone to focus on school. English, art, and biology. Quietly listening to the Cure and R.E.M. "You Are the Everything."

Writing poems and stories for no one to read. Making friends with the art teacher.

In my own small world, not worried about what anyone thought.

Sophomore year.

Ready for friends, maybe.

I wanted to have fun, feel safe, like the same stuff. Too much to ask?

Being judged by, judging by, music.

You like Depeche Mode? Which songs? Morrissey or the Smiths? Listening to Love and Rockets, Sting, Sinead O' Connor. "Just Like You Said It Would Be."

My mom and I could agree on Sting.

Some friends—the ones who cared more about my thoughts than my CD collection—and I would gather to discuss religion and politics, death and dreams. Hopes.

Hope for change. We can change. Change ourselves, change the world, change our lives. We were Philosophers.

I dreamed a future for myself that I could look forward to, move forward to.

Junior year.

Nine Inch Nails at Lollapalooza. "Head Like a Hole."

Not different enough for the uncool crowd. Not cool enough for the rest.

In my own little social bubble. Safe there. Somewhat content to not stand out.

Tried to like boys like they seemed to like me. I wasn't ready. I just wanted to write and draw and talk about comic books.

And make movies.

Video production class was art and writing in one. I found my home in scripts and cameras.

Then tragedy struck. Mom. The hospital. Weeks of missed school.

When I got back, I was sure everyone knew, was sure everyone was whispering about me. How tragic.

I didn't want them to know I was more different from all of them now. A mom at home who needed me to take care of her.

I didn't want to be different. I didn't want to be seen—crying.

The nurse let me lie in her office until the anxiety attacks passed.

Listening to Billy Joel and Tracy Chapman with my mom after school. "She's Got Her Ticket." Trying to teach her the lyrics she already knew.

Senior year.

Local-access TV. Working on the arts segment. My show. My production. My way forward. My way to change. Myself. The world. My life.

Listening to Living Color. Making a music video for "Cult of Personality" for my thesis theme: TV as a close-up medium. The editing room, the studio, my home away from.

Art was—everything.

College applications. Watching the mailbox. Waiting to unseal the envelopes that would seal my fate.

Acceptance letters. The ticket, my ticket, out.

Drove to graduation listening to "Life Is a Highway."

Kept on driving, going, moving on.

Left high school, my home, my friends, my mom—behind. I headed to the Big City to get a degree in making art, to learn to breathe freely.

A new life, new school, new me, with new people, new anxiety, new challenges. To face.

I took the bus home on the weekends.

Introduced mom to Tori Amos as we both tried to survive these "Little Earthquakes."

Chapter 6

A Christmas Story

My junior year of high school, when I was sixteen years old, I was working at the local five-and-dime store. It was three weeks before Christmas. I still had about an hour left on my shift when my older sister, Heather, showed up at work. She was crying. She said, "Mom's in the hospital. I don't know anything else."

I grabbed my stuff and we got in Heather's beat-up old Pinto. We drove to the hospital in silence.

We walked into the emergency room. The nurse told us to wait. Eventually a nurse or doctor came up to us and said, "You can go in and see your mother, but only one at a time, and not for very long."

My sister went in first. I sat there, alone in the hall, having no idea what was going on, trying very hard to stay calm. Heather was crying when she came out, but she didn't have time to say anything to me before I was ushered in.

When I went in the room, my mom was awake, lying in a bed, with tubes and machines and cables all over her. I was terrified by the sight but wanted to seem calm for her, because I thought that's what people did. So I just said, "Hi mom, how you doing?"

Mom didn't answer. She just shook her head and looked at the nurse.

The nurse said, "I know, you're trying to say it, but it won't come out."

Mom nodded. Why was she communicating with him and not me? What couldn't she tell me?

I said, "Mom, are you okay?"

She just shrugged and shook her head helplessly. I could feel the heat and tears building up, so I went over to her and hugged her carefully. After just a minute, the nurse told me it was time to leave.

I went back to waiting with my sister. I don't know how long we sat there, in ignorance and fear, until eventually a doctor finally came to talk to Heather and me. The only word I remember him saying was "stroke." It was like a gong banging in my head. Stroke. Stroke. Stroke.

Mom hadn't been afraid to give me the bad news. She didn't talk to me because she couldn't talk, because she'd had a stroke.

That night, Mom could hardly speak at all. In addition to dealing with her aphasia—the problem speaking—Mom couldn't read, write, or understand math. She lost most of her sight in one eye, her left hand shriveled up, and standing without falling over was difficult.

But by a few days later she could say, "I love you, Heather." And yes, it annoyed me that she remembered Heather's name first, but I forgave her. After all, when the doctor pointed to his pen and asked Mom to name it, she still called it a cow.

After about a week in the hospital, Mom was moved to an inpatient rehab center, and Heather and I returned to life as usual. Every day, while I went to high school and Heather to college, mom went back to elementary school. She had occupational therapy, physical therapy, recreational therapy, and speech therapy. And she made great progress.

Unfortunately, at night she shared a room with a horrible old woman who complained constantly about everything, including the fact that Mom had visitors.

And I hated visiting. As much as I loved my mom, I wanted out of there as soon as I got there. It smelled like urine and bleach, and the other residents, who were all suffering similar ailments as my mom's were scary to me. I hated that my mom was stuck there. I hated that my mom wasn't home.

But Mom always worried about us. When we'd go visit, she'd say, "Poor kids," like we were the ones suffering! We told her we were fine, but the truth is being on our own wasn't easy.

We had to do everything for ourselves. My dad had come to the hospital that first night, and then left again. My brother was away in college. He'd come home and stayed for a bit but had to go back and take finals. My mom's family was not around for us. Heather and I were on our own. We could cook—mac and cheese, TV dinners, Cookie Crisp cereal—and dress ourselves, but pretty much everything else had always been taken care of by Mom.

The first time Heather and I walked into the grocery store by ourselves, I felt this giant sob rise up in my chest and had to run out into the parking lot to cry. Not that shopping was so hard to do, but it didn't feel right without Mom there.

Somehow, Heather and I managed—buying groceries, paying bills, dealing with insurance and hospitals and homework. And then there was Christmas, just around the corner.

In a monumental failure of judgment, the rehab center decided to cheer the place up a bit by decorating and piping Christmas music over the loudspeakers all day long, and yes, it was as depressing as it sounds. If my mom hadn't been concerned about the upcoming holiday, she was now.

Unfortunately, they told us they wouldn't be able to release Mom for Christmas. In all likelihood, we'd have to spend

Christmas morning at the rehab center. And the horror of that prospect was driven home every time we visited her, as without fail they'd play "I'll Be Home for Christmas." You can count on that song to make you cry if the person you love won't, in fact, be home for Christmas.

Mom was the one who made Christmas. She cooked the cinnamon rolls, stuffed and hung the stockings, and bought and gave most of the presents. I really wasn't looking forward to this Christmas.

On one of my visits, Mom told me where she had some cash hidden. She wanted us to buy gifts for each other so it would still feel like Christmas on Christmas morning. Heather and I were barely holding things together financially, so we didn't spend Mom's cash on gifts. We spent it on groceries and bills.

But as much as I felt like a Grinch that year, one day we came home to find a Christmas tree beside our front door. Another time I found an unsigned Christmas card with cash in it in our mailbox. And even though neither Heather nor I was in the Christmas spirit, it felt like we had to "do" Christmas, if only because everyone wanted us to.

We decorated the tree, hung up the stockings, wrapped a few measly presents, and tried very hard to invoke the spirit of Christmas. And somehow, it worked. Possibly because it was time, possibly because she had improved more than anticipated, or possibly because of the season, on Christmas Eve, when we went to visit mom, the facility released her. They let us take her home for the holiday and to begin outpatient care after.

On Christmas morning, I woke up and made the cinnamon rolls. My brother and sister helped Mom out of bed and into her wheelchair. We gathered around the tree. There were a few presents under it, but that hardly mattered. Mom MADE that Christmas for us. She was alive. She was home. That was the best gift of all.

Chapter 7

A Love Story

EXT. WASHINGTON SQUARE PARK, NYC—DAY

JESSICA, 18 years old, dressed in oversized jeans, baggy T-shirt, and boots, walks through the park, enjoying the sunshine.

JESSICA (voiceover)

When I went to NYU film school, I learned that unlike real life, movies follow a formula. This is nowhere more apparent than in romantic movies. Act 1—Boy meets girl. Act 2—In the first half, they fall in love, and in the second half a problem arises that threatens the relationship. Act 3—They overcome the obstacle and are united by a kiss. If I were to write my first year of college as a romantic screenplay, it would go something like this.

Cut to

TITLE: Act 1—You had me at hello[1]

Cut to

INT. MEDIA SOLUTIONS OFFICE—DAY

Open on a small, dark office, walls lined with A/V equipment. In the center of the office is a lone desk. There are a few chairs crammed into corners around shelves, and one chair behind the desk.

JESSICA, 18 years old, dressed in oversized jeans, baggy T-shirt, and boots, sits nestled in a corner, staring at the man behind the desk.

SCOTT, 22 years old, wearing jeans, a black leather jacket over a white T-shirt, and wire-framed glasses, sits at the desk chewing on a pen and staring up at the ceiling.

> SCOTT
> You have to watch *Down by Law*. I can't believe you haven't seen it yet. It's Jarmusch's best. And anything with Tom Waits is amazing. You have his latest CD?

> JESSICA
> Uh, um. I don't think I know him.

> SCOTT
> What?! Start with *Closing Time*. I can lend you *Bone Machine* when you've heard his earlier stuff.

---

1   Crowe, C., 1996, *Jerry Maguire*, Tristar Pictures

SEAN, 20, walks into the room and starts talking to Scott. Jessica watches from her corner. Sean leaves, and Scott holds out some papers. Jessica takes them, reads them over, and starts gathering equipment off the shelves, loading a cart with it.

When the cart is fully loaded, Jessica lays the papers on top and turns to Scott, who is typing up something on the computer.

JESSICA

I'll be back in a bit. Can I get you anything while I'm out?

SCOTT (looking up and smiling)

A new life? A new job? Some direction, maybe?

JESSICA (smiling back)

I was thinking more like a coffee? But if you want direction, I am studying that now and should be able to direct you by the end of the year.

Scott smiles and goes back to typing. Jessica stares at him for a moment longer before pushing the cart out into the hall.

Cut to

TITLE: Act 2, Part 1 - You make me want to be a better man[2]

Cut to

INT. MEDIA SOLUTIONS OFFICE—Night

---

2   Brooks, J., 1997, *As Good as It Gets*, Sony Pictures Studios

Scott is sitting behind his desk, wearing the same black leather coat, but he's got a scarf wrapped around his neck. Jessica walks in with a TV cart, which she parks in the corner. She's dressed for winter, wearing jeans and an oversized wool sweater. She hands Scott some papers and lingers by his desk.

JESSICA
What are you doing this weekend?

SCOTT
I don't know. I do want to go see *Groundhog Day*. Harold Ramis is one of the best directors working today, and Bill Murray is great in everything. But other than that, I don't have any plans.

Jessica stands there awkwardly for a minute before Scott turns back to the work on his desk. His shoulders slump as he sees a piece of paper he didn't notice before.

SCOTT
I'm sorry. Before you sit down. Can you pick up a project in A17? I think that's the last thing left out at this point.

JESSICA (taking the paper from Scott)
Sure. Be back soon.

As Jessica walks out, she passes Sean and another guy coming back to the office with carts full of equipment.

Cut to

INT. MEDIA SOLUTIONS OFFICE—LATER THAT NIGHT

Jessica returns carrying a projector and screen. Scott gets up and takes the screen from her while she stores the projector on a shelf. Scott grabs a backpack from behind his desk.

JESSICA

Is that it?

SCOTT

Yup. We're done.

Jessica grabs a backpack from the corner and walks out into the hall with Scott.

INT. HALL OUTSIDE OFFICE—NIGHT

Scott stands closing and locking the office door. Jessica waits for him. They start walking down the hall together. Jessica fidgets with the straps on her backpack while Scott stares straight ahead. When they get to the front doors of the building, they both hesitate before heading out into the cold.

JESSICA (blurting out rapid fire)

Do you want to go see *Groundhog Day* with me?

SCOTT

Sure. I was going to go tomorrow at 8:00 pm, Third Ave.

JESSICA (letting out a big sigh)

Cool.

Cut to

EXT. TOMPKINS SQUARE—NIGHT

Jessica and Scott, wearing winter coats, walk into the square, talking animatedly.

SCOTT

Humor is the hardest thing to get right. I mean, people don't give funny actors enough credit, but no one else could've pulled that off. It's not just timing. It's all about the personality. The talent. It had to be Bill Murray.

Scott sits down on a bench, and Jessica sits next to him, smiling in agreement.

JESSICA

Totally. But the script was amazing too. That's the kind of movie. I want to make one day. Like funny and entertaining, but with meaning too.

SCOTT (looking introspective)

Don't take this the wrong way, but you make me want to get the hell out of media solutions.

Jessica stares at Scott, who is looking off into the distance, smiling, and blushing, and most definitely taking that the wrong way.

Cut to

TITLE: Act 2, Part 2—Nobody puts baby in the corner[3]

Cut to

INT. MEDIA SOLUTIONS OFFICE—NIGHT

Scott is sitting behind his desk and Jessica is at a chair in front, listening eagerly.

---

3   Ardolino, E., 1987, *Dirty Dancing*, Vestron Pictures

JESSICA PISCITELLI ROBINSON

SCOTT

I'm gonna make a movie this summer. Rent some equipment. Hire some friends. I just need to find a script that I can do on a budget.

Jessica's eyes go wide, as if a lightbulb has gone on in her head. She bites her lip.

Sean walks in, pushing a TV cart against the wall. He hands a paper to Scott.

SEAN

That it?

SCOTT

Yeah. I guess we're done.

SEAN

Good night.

Sean leaves quickly. Jessica doesn't move from her chair. She takes a deep breath and then blurts out . . .

JESSICA

Can we talk?

Scott blanches. He looks like he's been smacked. He grimaces and then responds.

SCOTT

Go ahead.

Jessica, seeing his response, blushes, and stammers out . . .

JESSICA

I was thinking that maybe, I mean, do you think that, would you ever consider reading my script?

Scott visibly relaxes, and lets out a little laugh.

SCOTT

Sure, but you gotta work on your pitch 'cause you almost gave me a heart attack.

Jessica, looking like she wants to cry, laughs as well.

JESSICA

If I was going to propose to you, I would have gotten down on one knee first.

Cut to

TITLE: Act 3—When you realize you want to spend the rest of your life with somebody, you want the rest of your life to start as soon as possible.[4]

Cut to

INT. MEDIA SOLUTIONS OFFICE—NIGHT

Scott is sitting at his desk, in jeans and T-shirt, no jacket, staring at the ceiling. Jessica is sitting in the corner again, in jeans and T-shirt, reading a book. Scott lets out a loud sigh and sits up.

---

4   Reiner, R., 1989, *When Harry Met Sally*, Columbia Pictures

SCOTT

All right, you can go.

Jessica looks up from her book.

JESSICA

You don't need me to wait?

SCOTT

Nah. Nothing's gonna happen in the next fifteen minutes. Enjoy your summer break a few minutes early.

Jessica puts her book in her backpack and stands by Scott's desk.

JESSICA

Doing anything cool this summer?

SCOTT

Just working here. Aargh. I gotta get out of here. I gotta do something with my life.

JESSICA

So, you're not making a movie then?

Scott, as if remembering something, digs around in his desk drawer and pulls out a script. He hands it to Jessica.

SCOTT

Sorry I didn't get around to reading it. See you in the fall.

Scott gets up and hugs Jessica, not tightly. She walks out of the office, a look of hurt on her face.

Cut to

INT. CRAMPED NYC BEDROOM—LATER THAT NIGHT

Jessica walks into her room, dropping her backpack on her bed. She digs out her script and tosses it on her desk. As she does so, a postcard falls out. On the front is a picture of Alfred Hitchcock and Andy Warhol. On the back, a handwritten note.

INSERT NOTE: I've been meaning to write this a long time. I've been meaning to do a lot of things for a long time. Keep this card and imagine I had written something meaningful and profound, something you would have thought about and disagreed with. Something like it doesn't matter where you're going so long as you know where you've been. Love Scott.

Jessica stares at the note for a long time before tucking it back into her script and putting both into her desk drawer.

Cut to

INT. MEDIA SOLUTIONS OFFICE—DAY

Scott is sitting behind the desk. There's a guy sitting in Jessica's usual spot. Jessica walks in. Scott looks up, confused to see her.

SCOTT
You're not working today, are you?

JESSICA
No, I was in the neighborhood. Thought I'd swing by.

The guy from the corner gets up. Scott hands him his papers and he grabs some equipment before leaving. Scott goes back to work while Jessica stands awkwardly in front of his desk.

                    JESSICA
    I wanted to thank you for the postcard.

Scott responds, not looking up.

                    SCOTT
    Yeah, no problem.

                    JESSICA
    I don't go home for a couple days. Did you want to hang
    out, or something?

                    SCOTT (finally looking at Jessica)
    Uh, I can't. Sorry. See you next year?

Jessica looks crestfallen.

                    JESSICA
    Yeah. Sure. Have a good summer.

Scott goes back to work. Jessica walks out.

                                            Cut to

EXT. WASHINGTON SQUARE PARK—DAY

As Jessica walks through the park, she starts walking more briskly,
more confidently and by the time she walks out of the park, she
is smiling and enjoying the sunshine.

                    JESSICA (voiceover)
    I didn't know what Scott thought about me, if he

thought anything at all. I only knew that I couldn't do it anymore. I couldn't wait for him and hope for him and wish that he secretly loved me but was too shy or scared or whatever to tell me. He could've told me a million times and he hadn't. I had to get away from him before I went crazy.

When it came time to choose hours for the fall semester, I shifted my calendar around so that I would work with Scott as little as possible.

If I had written this screenplay to be made into a movie, when Scott found out that he wasn't going to see me anymore, he would've realized that he couldn't live without me. He would have come into work early one day, surprising me at the end of my shift, swept me off my feet, kissed me, and carried me out of the media factory. But one thing I learned at NYU is that unlike the movies, real life doesn't follow a formula.

FADE TO BLACK

Chapter 8

The Graduate

As I stood for hours in the warm May downpour in the middle of Washington Square Park, right next to the fountain, and waited for Robert De Niro to speak at my college graduation, I wondered if the nearly $100,000 worth of debt I'd gotten myself into was worth it.

I knew from the time I was fifteen or so that I wanted to direct movies. Since there was no guidebook on how to break into the feature film industry, I decided I needed to attend the best film school in the country—NYU's Tisch School of the Arts.

NYU was a tad bit pricey. Through a combination of my dad maxing out the loans he could get, me maxing out the loans and credit cards I could get, a tiny scholarship I'd earned, and me working two jobs, I managed to just make my tuition payments each semester. I kept telling myself the stress and debt will be worth it when I graduate from the same school as Spike Lee and Marty Scorsese—if you're from NY you can call him Marty.

College was costing me dearly, so I worked hard to achieve dean's list every semester. Other kids didn't worry so much.

They didn't need good grades. They didn't even need to do well, as many of them had relatives in the industry, high up in the industry. And others just had money, lots of it, so that they didn't even need to borrow the NYU film equipment to make their shorts—twenty-year-olds with tens of thousands of dollars in film equipment—or use other students as crew. Seriously, some of them hired professional DPs and sound engineers and actually paid actors to be in their student films! No one pays actors.

I'd like to say I tried hard not to judge the other kids, but listening to stories of them going out every night while I was at work, or hearing about their vacations skiing in the Alps or scuba diving in the Caymans while I vacationed by walking around the city—because walking is free—made it hard not to feel a tad bit jealous, and maybe a little superior. You see, while they went to dinner with Jonathan Demme or Peter Bogdanovich, I got to suffer for my art, and isn't that what true artists do?

But as I stood in the middle of Washington Square Park, waiting for Bobby De Niro to take the stage—if you live in NY you can call him Bobby-I kept thinking, *Finally! I am finally done having to work twice as hard as everyone around me. Things are equal now because I have a degree from NYU. Who wouldn't want to hire an NYU film school graduate?*

As Bobby was about to walk to the podium to get his honorary degree, a professional photographer tried to gain an advantageous spot by climbing on top of the fountain wall. To do that, he had to pull a student off the wall. And then said student got mad and pulled the photographer off. And in between punches I heard the photographer yelling, "I'm getting paid to take pictures," and I heard the kid yelling, "It's my graduation," and I couldn't help but side with the kid. After all, I knew how much this graduation cost.

Seeing as he was surrounded by about thirty thousand students, the photographer gave up and skulked away. All was calm beneath the pouring rain as Bobby stepped up to the mic.

He said something about how he wasn't the important one here, the PhD giving the commencement speech was. The crowd laughed at that and demanded "speech, speech, speech." He was Bobby De Niro, not some dumb doctor.

So, perhaps to appease us, or perhaps because he'd actually prepared this, he begrudgingly added "Break a leg" before walking offstage. He is famous for his acting, not his writing.

I don't remember anything that the doctor guy said, and ultimately what stood out the most about my graduation in the park was the fistfight. But, at least, unlike most other people who have graduated college, I can remember, word for word, one of the speeches made that day. How could I forget "Break a leg"?

I did go to work in the feature film industry. The first person who hired me was impressed by my BFA. Grades matter. Stay in school, kids. I started off working as an office PA. I worked hard, long hours and kept telling anyone who would listen that I wanted to work on set. It didn't take long.

On my first movie set, on my very first day, the assistant director pulled me aside and said, "Just because you went to NYU doesn't mean you're the director. You're gonna have to work hard." I didn't have a problem with that, other than I thought it unnecessary to say, but we moved on, and once he'd gotten to know me, to know what a good worker I was, we got along fine and I put the whole conversation behind me.

On my second movie, the gaffer asked what seemed like an innocent question: "How'd you get into the industry?" I answered, "I went to NYU." From that moment on, he proceeded to treat me like I thought I was too good for everything, even though I worked as hard as everyone else, without complaint. Anytime he needed anything from me he'd say, "Can I get a hot battery or are you too good to get it for me? Can I get some coffee or is that beneath you? You gonna pick up that garbage or you want an assistant to do it for you?"

NYU graduates did have a reputation for going to the best

film school in the country. Sadly, we also had a reputation for thinking we were better than everyone else.

Crew on movies work very hard for very little money and aren't partial to entitled rich kids. I should've fit right in, but my costly education was a black cloud over me. After that second movie, I stopped telling people that I went to NYU, and people stopped expecting the worst of me.

I worked hard, as I'd always done, and in three years in the film industry, I went from the lowest position on set to being offered a job as a second AD, just one step from the top of the ladder. My ego was thrilled, but my brain had other ideas. I turned the job down and left the film industry, for a long list of reasons, the biggest being that I realized that not actually being a rich kid myself, I would probably never make it to the top of the ladder.

Sometimes you can pull a *Blair Witch* and get there from outside the system. Sometimes you can work hard as a first AD for twenty years and make enough powerful friends that someone lets you call the shots. But mostly, getting a position above the line, like director, is more about who you know and how much money you can access and not so much about how hard you work.

I left the film industry and began working for a commercial firm and then started my own video production company not long after, where I get to direct every video. And in the world of business, where things boil down to ROI, your work ethic matters, as does your reputation. Which is why whenever I meet with a new prospect, one who doesn't yet know what a great worker I am, I always make sure to brag—just a little—about graduating with honors from the top film school in the country. Sometimes I even mention how Bobby De Niro spoke at my graduation.

Chapter 9

Face Value

What do you think a young woman's face is worth? I can give you an exact amount. I had mine appraised once.

I was twenty-three years old, working in New York City. Despite the glamorous lifestyle of NYC, I didn't wear makeup, I dressed in jeans and T-shirts, and I hadn't had my hair professionally cut in the seven years I'd lived there. Partly because I was broke, but mostly because I was so sick of the constant catcalls that I did whatever I could to minimize the amount of attention I drew to myself.

I was working as a production assistant in the feature film industry. I had just been sent on a run by the wardrobe department to pick up some suits for an actor. I had them in hand. They were so big I had to hold them over my head to keep them from dragging on the ground. I was standing on the corner of Fifth Avenue and Sixtieth Street, on the Central Park side, waiting for the light to change so I could cross the street. It was winter, and I was looking around, thinking how weirdly empty it was. There didn't seem to be any cars or other people around.

It was peaceful. Unusual for NY.

So, it was somewhat surprising that when the light changed and I began walking across Fifth Ave, a car seemed to come out of nowhere—a New York City cab—and it looked like it was heading right toward me. I just had time to think, *He's gonna hit me.*

When I opened my eyes, my face was inches from the pavement. This pool of blood was rapidly expanding as this waterfall of blood poured into it. Someone was screaming. It was like a scene from a war movie. Then a passerby, another person I hadn't noticed, came up to me in the street and put his hand on my shoulder. When I looked up at him, I stopped screaming.

He stayed with me until the cops came, and they stayed with me until the ambulance came and took me to a New York City hospital emergency room, which was not as bad as I had imagined it would be. There were maybe only twelve people in the beds around me. The nurse pulled the curtains closed, and then she sort of rolled me this way and that to get me out of my clothes and into one of those thin hospital gowns. I had a big neck brace on from my trip on the ambulance, so I wasn't getting jostled too much.

The nurse covered me with one of those useless hospital sheets and set to work on my head. I couldn't feel what she was doing—everything was numb—but it seemed like she was cleaning out a wound on my forehead with a spray bottle. Then she set up a sort of quarantine tent over the top of my head before leaving me alone.

I was terrified that the reason I couldn't feel anything was that I was paralyzed. But the nurse came back quickly with a shiny silver bowl, which she put under my butt, and she said, "All right, we're gonna need a urine sample to be sure you're not pregnant before we can give you an X-ray."

I said, "Well, there's no concern about pregnancy because I'm still a virgin."

Unimpressed, she said, "That's great, dear. We still need a urine sample."

Then she stood there waiting. And even though I really wanted to find out if my neck was broken, I couldn't go with her standing there.

I said, "I'm going to need a little bit more time."

She left me my space. I laid there, worried about my ability to ever walk again and trying to go to the bathroom despite all the voices coming from just the other side of the curtains. A doctor came through the curtains, up to my bedside, and started talking to me. I was still thinking about my back, so it took me a while to catch up because what he was talking about was my face.

He said, "Now, we could sew you up here in the emergency room. We can take care of that for you. You're gonna have a scar either way. But we happen to have the finest vascular surgeon in the country on staff right here at this hospital. She's in surgery at the moment, but I took the liberty of speaking with her and telling her we have a young woman with a facial wound, and she's agreed to squeeze you into her schedule at the end of the day. That is, of course, if you're willing to wait."

His bedside manner was so dry I couldn't help but reply a little sarcastically, "Well, gee, I mean I gotta check my schedule. You know what? Actually, I think it's opened up. So yeah, I can wait."

He had no sense of humor, so he didn't smile. He just said, flatly, "Great." He continued, "Now, do you have a lawyer?"

I said, "I am twenty-three years old and broke. So, no. No lawyer on staff."

He had no sense of humor, so he didn't smile. He just said, "Great." He handed me a business card and added, "Call my guy. He'll take good care of you."

His sales quota apparently met, he walked away, leaving me holding the business card, looking for a pocket on my hospital gown.

The nurse came by a little while later and took the business card and put it with my personal effects. She said, "All right, did you pee?"

I said, "I don't think I can."

"All right, I'll go get the catheter."

Before she walked away, I said, "You know what? Actually, I think I can do it." And I did. And I wasn't pregnant and my neck wasn't broken.

A few hours later, the finest vascular surgeon in the country showed up, and she put her face over mine and got to work. As she worked, she talked, which was good because it is very weird having your face operated on while you are conscious. She explained to me that when my face met Fifth Avenue, I left behind not only skin but also tissue and muscle the size of a softball. She was going to do her best to close the wound, but there wasn't enough muscle for her to pull closed across my forehead. I would always have an area of my forehead that just wouldn't move.

I couldn't help but say, "Awesome. It's like free Botox!"

She had a sense of humor, so she laughed.

My dad picked me up from the hospital. When he came up to my hospital bed and saw the state of my face, he had to turn away so I wouldn't see him crying. The whole time I'd been in the hospital, no one had given me a mirror. I could only imagine.

When I got home, I looked in the mirror. I had bandages on my head over the wound on my forehead. My cheek and eye, and many parts of my body, were black and blue and green and yellow.

I spent two weeks recuperating, trying to get physically and mentally prepared to go back to work. I called that lawyer. I didn't know any others. He agreed there was a case and took me on as his client.

When I went back to the doctor for a checkup, they took the bandages off, leaving a jagged, puffy line across my forehead, with horrid black stitches. When the stitches came out, I had an ugly red scar on my forehead.

I went back to work in the city, and it felt like everywhere I went there was this red beacon of unwanted attention. I just wanted to hide my face. Some days I stepped into doorways just to hide for a few minutes, to try to catch my breath, to stamp down the rising anxiety.

The anxiety built up, and a couple weeks later, I couldn't take it anymore. For the first time since moving to NY, I went and got my hair professionally done.

When I sat in the chair, the hairdresser said, "What do you want?"

I said, "I don't care as long as you cover this."

She proceeded to give me bangs, and I proceeded to sob through the whole haircut because it felt like defeat. The haircut was traumatic—not only for me but for the poor lady cutting my hair—but we got through it, and I've pretty much had bangs ever since.

About a year later, my lawyer called and said that the cab company's lawyers were ready to meet. I went into the city and met with my lawyer in the lobby of the building about fifteen minutes before going up to meet with them.

He said, "How are you doing?"

I said, "Well, you know, my back's really messed up. I've been in traction and physical therapy and still seeing a chiropractor twice a week."

He said, "No. Soft tissue damage doesn't pay. How's your face? Can you move your bangs?"

So, I did and he said, "Does that ever look any worse?"

I raised my eyebrows in response, and he said, "Yeah, like that. Can you do that the whole time we're up there?"

When I raise my eyebrows, that part of my forehead that has no muscle becomes a crater. I figured I wasn't gonna get anything for my back, so I might as well get as much as possible for my face. My lawyer and I walked into the room. Twelve guys in various shades of gray suits stared at me for five minutes while I held my eyebrows up.

Three weeks later, I got a check in the mail for the sum total value of what a young woman's face was worth.

Over the past twenty-plus years, there have been very few days without back or neck pain. I've been to doctors, surgeons, taken medication, gotten acupuncture, seen holistic practitioners, bought devices, and done all the exercises. But physical injuries don't age well.

Conversely, as I've gotten older, I've stopped feeling like everyone is looking at me, stopped caring even if they are. My back was what was truly damaged in the accident, yet it was only my face that was considered of value. The value of $40,000.

Chapter 10

The Talk

"Does it hurt?"

"Does what hurt?"

"You know, *it*. Does *it* hurt? Like, the first time."

I was eight years old and I had just asked my mom about losing my virginity.

She smiled, as if recalling some happy memory, and said, "No. Not if you're in love. If he cares about you and you care about him, it doesn't hurt. In fact, it feels good."

Unfortunately, that wasn't the only time we talked about *it*. When I hit the more appropriate age of twelve or thirteen, my mom stopped editing herself and told me many horrifying things about sex, horrifying because they were about my mom having sex. She loved sex, and wanted me to grow up to enjoy it as well.

As a grown woman, I am grateful that she instilled in me the idea that sex is something a woman should enjoy. As I was growing up, however, I learned to tune out most of what my mom said about sex. But the talk we'd had when I was eight stuck with me, became my guide. I wanted my first time to be with someone who cared about me. I hadn't realized that was such a high bar to set, yet at twenty-three years old, I was still looking.

I was working as a production assistant in the film industry in New York. One night, I went to a wrap party for a movie I'd worked on for only a week. Wrap parties meant free alcohol, and I was young. Plus, I liked the crew and wanted to have a night out with the guys before we all moved on to the next movie.

At around midnight, after I'd probably had two or three too many, Jim came up to me at the bar and handed me a drink. I'd never worked with him on any other movies, so I'd only known him for six days. There wasn't much time to talk during work, but whenever we had, he seemed nice. He was soft-spoken, tall and thin and had a boy-next-door sort of charm.

I probably didn't need to take another shot, but why not? I took the glass from Jim, and we both drank. Then he pulled me onto the dance floor. He started swinging me around jitterbug style, and after maybe a minute, I started to get really dizzy. It was like the world around me was blurring out of focus and I couldn't find my balance. Jim pulled me off the dance floor and out of the bar, without giving me a chance to say goodbye to anyone.

I confess, much of the rest of the night is unclear to me. The moments I do recall feel distant, like scenes from a movie. But there are gaps, like an unfinished movie. Between each scene, there is blackness.

Cut.

Jim and I were in a cab. I noticed we were riding uptown. I said, "I live in Brooklyn."

Jim put his hand on my leg and told me, "It's okay."

Cut.

Jim pushed me into his apartment, hand on the small of my back. He didn't turn his lights on, and I couldn't see. He kept his hand there, nudging me through the apartment and into his bedroom. As soon as the door closed behind him, he pulled my dress off over my head. It wasn't passionate. We weren't making out and ripping each other's clothes off. He just took my dress off as if it were in his way.

Cut.

We were in his bed. Jim was propped on one arm, holding up a condom. I waved it away, saying, "Whoa, we're not gonna need that."

He smiled, threw it on the ground, and said, "Awesome."

Cut.

Jim was leaning over me, hand between my legs. I said, "I'm a virgin."

Normally, that frightened guys away. Jim just said, "That's great."

I said, "I don't want to do this."

Cut.

Jim was on top of me. He said, "Ready?"

Before I could answer, he was inside me. There was a pinch. It hurt.

Cut.

Jim was lying next to me, snoring. I climbed out of bed as quietly as possible, but ended up falling to the ground. The bed was high, stacked on dresser drawers.

Jim continued to snore. I stumbled around the dark room trying to find my underwear, bra, dress, purse, and shoes amid his possessions, scattered across the floor. I didn't turn on the light. I didn't want to wake him.

I got dressed and found his bathroom. As I pulled my underwear down, blood smeared along my thigh. The sight of the blood hit me—I was no longer a virgin. I sat on the toilet and cried until I started to worry that he might wake up and find me.

Cut.

I walked out of his apartment and downstairs onto the street, which is when I realized I had no idea where I was. It was 4:00 a.m. I was still woozy, in last night's dress, and I hadn't brought money for a cab. What could I do? I walked toward an avenue, looking for a subway stop.

Cut.

I got home around 5:00 a.m. and cried all weekend. I kept playing those scenes back, over and over in my head. Trying to make sense of them. Trying to understand what had happened. I felt ashamed, guilty, confused. I didn't understand what had happened, but I was sure I hadn't wanted it. I hadn't meant to give it up to a guy I hardly knew, a guy I was pretty sure didn't care about me. But I hadn't stopped it. Why hadn't I said stop? Why hadn't I fought, or yelled? But I hadn't. I had no one to blame but myself. It was my fault.

I needed my mom. I called her, still crying, and said, "I didn't want it to happen. I didn't mean for it to happen."

Mom said, "It's all right. It's over now."

I said, "But I don't understand. It felt wrong."

She said, "I love you. You're going to be okay. Try to put it behind you and move on."

I tried to put it behind me. I tried to move on. But the next guy - the first guy who actually cared about me - when we tried to make love, I couldn't stop crying. He said, "Jess. I'm so sorry. Did I hurt you?" And I couldn't tell him it wasn't him who hurt me.

About ten years later, a few of my girlfriends came over to help me settle into my new, postdivorce townhouse in Northern Virginia. We were all single, and so, of course, we started talking about sex, which led to a discussion of our first times. One of my friends had a wonderful experience with a guy she loved. The two others had a similar experience to mine. One had been unconscious in her dorm when it happened. The other had been with her boyfriend and told him she wasn't ready. He hadn't listened. When the three of us shared our experiences, none of us used the word "rape."

A few weeks later, I was watching TV alone, and some dumb movie came on. I watched it anyway. It was a bad-movie kind of a day. There was a scene in which this teenage girl, the protagonist's daughter, went into a bar. Some guy she didn't know gave her a drink, and even though she didn't know him, she drank it. She started getting woozy, and the guy pulled her out of the bar, into the back of a cab, and back to his apartment. Then he was on top of her, and I was on the floor sobbing. I realized that what happened to her was the same as what had happened to me. The movie was clear on what happened to her—she was raped. For the first time, I realized I had been raped.

I wish I could say that that was all I needed. That I cried it out and all that guilt I had carried for that decade just washed away with the knowledge that it hadn't been my fault. But it's more complicated than that. I may not be carrying the guilt, but the shame of it is harder to wash away. And even another decade later, it still hurts.

When I called my mom the weekend I lost my virginity and told her what had happened, she told me it was over. She didn't say, "It wasn't your fault." She didn't say, "What he did to you was wrong." She said it was over. I don't blame my mom. She loved me. She wished I wasn't in pain. She wanted me to bury what had happened and move on, the way so many women have done. That's what women do. They hold the event within, in a knot of shame within themselves, and don't talk to anyone about it. It's been over twenty years now, and I'm okay, but it's not over.

When I became a mom, first to a daughter and later to a son, all those cheesy things they tell you about becoming a parent became true for me. I no longer think about myself first. I think about my kids first. I would do anything to keep my kids from getting hurt. It may not seem a big thing, but I would unbury my own shame and discomfort a thousand times over if it meant saving them from the same.

Soon, we will need to have the talk. I will tell both my kids about the birds and the bees, about using protection, about double standards, about respecting your partner's body, and your own. And I will tell them my mom's advice. It's still good advice. If you care about the other person and they care about you, it shouldn't hurt, and it should feel good. I will also tell them the story of my rape, and hope that that's enough.

But if either of them ever comes to me and says, "I was drunk. I didn't want to. It hurt," then I will take them in my arms and say, "I love you. You're going to be okay. And know that this was not your fault."

Chapter 11

SCUBA Lessons

When I was in my early twenties, I fell in love, and for the very first time, he loved me back. And boy, did I fall hard. So hard it was like I had the breath knocked out of me, like I was drowning in my love for Jake. The only thing I thought I knew about love was that you were supposed to do everything within your power to make the other person happy. And Jake was happy to accept this arrangement, so long as he didn't have to reciprocate.

For our first birthday together—I mean our first important birthday together, Jake's—I decided to make Jake's dream a reality. He'd always wanted to be an oceanographer, but he'd never gotten beyond watching Shark Week, so I signed him up for scuba diving lessons. And since this was love, I signed myself up as well.

When I gave Jake his gift, he said "Wow, thanks." Then he did a kind of double take and said, "Wait. You're gonna do this with me?"

"Yeah, I want to be there for you."

"Well, try to keep up."

Scuba certification comes in three stages. The first is classroom. They teach the theory of how to breathe underwater first so that when you actually attempt it you won't die, you know, in theory. Jake and I passed the written tests and advanced to stage two—the pool.

It was when I was standing at the side of the Olympic-size pool that I started to get a little nervous. The instructor was explaining that in order to pass, we'd have to swim four laps in said pool. I started to think that maybe this hadn't been the best idea because, you see, I can't swim. I never learned how.

Nobody else in the class seemed to have a problem with this. It's almost as if people who sign up for scuba lessons already know how to swim. I don't know. But I was already there so might as well dive—or belly flop—right in.

Jake finished his laps quickly. I could see him standing by the side of the pool, rolling his eyes and looking at his waterproof watch as I became the last swimmer left. Fortunately, there was no time limit, so I was able to doggie paddle my way to passing. And I was really proud of myself for that, even if Jake did walk out of the building ahead of me, not bothering to look back as I tried to keep up.

We moved on to the final stage—open water. We flew down to the Florida Keys for the test. It was the morning of the dive when we were standing on the dock and I was looking at the boat and, really, at what was beyond the boat when I had that second twinge of apprehension. You see, I'm terrified of water. I mean I can handle a Jacuzzi just fine. I took a shower this morning, I swear. But open water, the kind you can't see the end of—that's another story.

I grew up at the shore. That's what we call the beach in NJ. And one of my earliest memories is of my mom warning me about this monster called the undertow. If you go into the ocean over your ankles, the undertow will grab you, drag you under, and pull you out to Mexico. My mom liked to tease, so I assumed she was joking, but then I went in the ocean. The undertow got me, pulled me under, and I almost drowned. The next summer, the same thing happened. By the time I was five I stopped going in over my ankles.

Standing on the dock with Jake, I felt rooted to the spot. I turned to Jake and said, "I don't think I can get on that boat." I told him about the undertow and the ankles and how I didn't think it was such a good idea that I should go in over them. He just rolled his eyes.

"Why do you always have to ruin everything for me? You know I need a buddy to dive with."

Which is mostly true. I was trying to make Jake happy, and he wanted me to go with him, so I got on the boat. And then the boat started heading out into the middle of the ocean, and nobody seemed to have a problem with that! It's almost as if people who sign up for scuba diving lessons expect to go into the ocean!

Then, about three minutes into the boat ride, I realized there was another reason I hadn't been on a boat in about twenty years—apparently, I get seasick, really easily. I started feeling nauseous and I guess I started turning green, 'cause Jake turned away from me, as if my misery was contagious. But our scuba instructor, whom I'm gonna call Zen, 'cause he was, well, he came over to me, put a warm hand on my shoulder, and said, "Look out on the horizon. Find a spot that isn't moving and focus on it."

I looked out at the horizon—and there was no spot that wasn't moving! Everything was swaying back and forth, including the contents of my stomach. I was holding my breath for the moment the boat stopped.

When we finally dropped anchor, I was determined to be one of the first people in the water. I figured if I could just get off the boat and into the water, I'd stop swaying and then this nausea would go away. It was good. The lurching feeling in my stomach distracted me from the fact that I was about to die when the undertow dragged me out to Mexico.

The scuba instructors jumped in first, and then I followed right after—holding my mask and jumping off the back of the boat.

In the water, I noticed a few things right away. When you are floating on top of the ocean, the swaying doesn't stop. I couldn't focus on the horizon anymore because now I couldn't even see it. I was in way over my ankles, and there was no place to put my feet down!

I think I reacted as rationally as one might expect. I freaked out, started hyperventilating and doggie paddling furiously, trying to get back on the boat.

Zen reached out and grabbed the back of my tank, turning me around to face him. He said, "Okay?"

Pull it together. You're doing this to make Jake happy. Breathe.

I started to respond but decided to be absolutely clear and just throw up instead.

Zen and I watched my vomit get dragged out to Mexico, and then he repeated, "Okay?"

I looked around for Jake, but he'd already descended. He hadn't waited. This was up to me.

"Okay"

"It will be calmer below."

"Great."

Zen smiled reassuringly and added, "If you need to vomit while we're down there, make sure you blow it through your mouthpiece or you'll run out of air."

And with that, he left me.

I did not want to throw up while I was down there, so I decided to rinse the taste out of my mouth with some seawater. You know, kind of a palate cleanser. Problem was that I was still near the back of the boat. Fun fact, oil induces vomit.

And if you think watching your vomit wash out to Mexico twice in one day is fun, you have really got to try scuba diving with vomit and oil in your mouth. There is nothing quite like every breath you take being flavored by oily chunks.

But you know what? I grabbed onto the anchor line and pulled myself down. On the bottom, even though I could see Zen and Jake and the others, the only sound was that of my own breathing. I felt as if the water was a wall isolating me from everyone else.

The sun shone through enough so we could see the tropical fish, the nearby reef, and Zen, showing us the final test—pacing your breathing to level yourself so you could float in perfect balance, like Zen.

I was not good at it. I floated up to standing and dropped down to face-plant, but I was finally able to breathe just right so that I hung there, in balance, for long enough to earn the universal sign of approval from Zen. He gave me a big "okay."

And hey, I didn't drown. In fact, despite, or maybe because of, feeling alone with myself, I loved every second of being down there. I felt so happy there.

Back in our hotel room, I was hungover from the seasickness, so I just curled up in a ball. Jake left me alone while I tried to sink into the bed. When he came back, he was so excited he didn't notice how sick I felt.

He said, "Guess what? There's a night dive, tonight. We're totally doing it."

I pushed myself up, put my bare feet on the hard floor, took a deep breath, and said, "No, we are not."

When I finally left Jake for good, I took my newly unearthed sense of my own happiness, and I took my scuba certification.

Chapter 12

That's a Wrap

I'd wanted to make movies since I was a kid. And after graduating from film school, my dream came true. I started working as a PA—a production assistant, which is basically the bottom of the ladder in the film industry—but I was just excited to be on the ladder. So excited I never complained about the long hours—we averaged eighteen-hour days, six days a week—or the crappy pay: when you did the math, it was under ten dollars an hour with no benefits. I was living the dream.

On movies, there are two groups of people: above the line and below the line. Below-the-line personnel are all those people whose names are really small and fly by really quickly in the credits: most of the crew. Above-the-line people are the creatives and the money people: producers, directors, and, of course, the actors.

And maybe because I didn't complain, or maybe because I seemed to have that special something, I moved up quickly to the next rung on the ladder: first-team PA. As first-team PA, I was in charge of the stars—or, you know, had to deal with them.

I worked with a lot of really mean actors and a few sweet ones, but there is one who stood out from all the rest as, shall we say, the most interesting.

It was 1999. I was working on this low-budget made-for-TV movie about a boys' school in the ghetto and the tough yet warmhearted priest who worked tirelessly to give those boys a better life. The priest was played by Mickey Rourke, slumming it on TV before it was cool for movie stars to do that.

As first-team PA, I greeted the actors when they arrived, gave them their scenes, saw if there was anything I could do to make their day that much brighter, and then escorted them to hair and makeup while wardrobe loaded their first outfit.

I had a lot of help, in addition to the other members of the first-team crew (the hair, makeup, and wardrobe people). There was the second AD, who set the schedule; the teamsters, who delivered the actors; and the PAs, who made coffee and food runs. And to coordinate, I had my handy-dandy walkie-talkie.

I said, "Go to two." (two was the channel we went to for private conversation) "Go to two. Mickey has arrived and is on his bus."

The second AD said, "Copy that. Back to one."

I loved working on movies because, you know, I was fulfilling a lifelong dream. But what I really loved was playing with walkie-talkies!

"Go to two. Did you see that guy try to walk into shot? I know, right? Oops, gotta go. Back to one."

On a perfect day, everything went smoothly—and the actors were happy. However, I quickly learned that when dealing with actors, perfect days were few and far between.

Mickey was never mean to me, but he was a bit of a challenge. For example, every day for three weeks, we shot in the same location. And for three weeks, Mickey's bus was parked in the same place. And for three weeks, Mickey just had to come out of his bus, turn left, and walk twenty yards to set. And, of course, everyday it was like flagging down a 747.

"Mickey. Over here. This way, Mickey. We're going to set. This way." Even with a group of us directing and pointing, he'd still sometimes wander off in the wrong direction.

He complicated my job further by driving the hair person nuts. Mickey would arrive on-site every day with his hair already perfectly coiffed in a sort of Elvis do—I know what you're thinking: *Very priest-like.* The hair guy was not allowed to touch it. After the first scene was completed, Mickey would go back to his bus to wait the three or four hours until he was needed again and, apparently, take a nap. This wouldn't have been a problem, or even something I would have known about, if not for the exceptional amount of hair gel he employed, so that when we'd walk back to set, his hair resembled a very priestly half mohawk.

The wardrobe person was not Mickey's biggest fan either. This was a low-budget movie, so funds for costumes were limited. In this case, Mickey's costume was a priest outfit: collar, black shirt, black pants. At the end of each day, when Mickey wrapped, instead of going to his bus and changing like actors normally do, he went to his ride and headed home. Which, you know, wouldn't have been so bad if he had ever brought any of his costumes back. But he didn't. Not once. After a week, we were out of priest outfits, and the wardrobe department threw up its hands and said let him wear his own clothes to set.

For Mickey's remaining scenes, the lighting department tried to keep the shots dim, the camera department tried to frame the shots creatively, and Mickey just did Mickey, showing up to set each day playing a priest who really loved to wear blue velvet running suits.

But the most interesting Mickey event came on an evening near the end of production when I was forced to call in the big gun: the movie's producer.

"Does anyone have eyes on Michael? Tell him to go to two please. Yeah, hi, um, Mickey's not gonna come to set today.

Nope, he won't tell me. Yep, he's on his bus. Copy that. Back to one."

Michael marched over to Mickey's bus looking like a teacher about to give a little kid a good scolding. When he stepped off the bus, he looked like a grandpa who's just realized his grandkid has been spoiled beyond saving.

"Get me the teamster captain."

I stood by and watched this above-the-line battle play out. It was the middle of the night. We were in the middle of the Bronx, and teamsters were scattered to the four corners.

Nothing I had learned about moviemaking in college had prepared me for this. I understood hard work, long hours, and scraping by until you reached the top. But I couldn't understand why someone with one of the coolest jobs on set, and probably anywhere, someone who was probably making more in that one job than I would in my life, thought he could put an entire production on hold, putting at risk the livelihoods of not only us below-the-line peons but also the above-the-line guys: all for some stupid whim.

Maybe because he was getting away with doing exactly that. It was a few hours of everyone sitting around not working before I got the call.

"Jessica, go to two."

"On two."

"The teamsters found one. Bringing it to you now."

"Copy that. Back to one."

The teamster handed me the package, and I knocked on Mickey's door. He opened the door, and as soon as he saw it, he was a happy little boy. He practically cried with delight as he held his new Chihuahua. And that was it. That was all it took. One Chihuahua. Mickey got his new dog settled on his bus, walked with me to set, and we were able to finish the movie.

As I looked around at the faces of the crew, at all these grown men and women hugging one another in relief because they would, in fact, be allowed to see their families soon, I thought, This is movie making. It didn't matter how hard you worked or how smart or passionate you were; your livelihood depended on some spoiled kid getting all their demands met. And I realized that if getting to the top of the ladder meant acquiring Chihuahuas for a living, then maybe I should find a better ladder.

Copy that. Back to one.

Chapter 13

Eurydice and Me

When I look back from this distant place in my life, it's apparent that Jake and I were fighting from the very beginning of our relationship. I think it's because I wanted him more than he wanted me. He'd never had a girlfriend, and he told me he'd never wanted one. I'd never had a boyfriend, but I wanted him. I went after him. And when I finally got him, I just wanted to hold on to him.

We were in this weird situation in which he lived in New Jersey and I lived in Brooklyn. He was underemployed and I was overemployed. I was working six days a week in the NY film industry, and I could only see him one day of the week. All week long I just waited for that one day. Then, when I finally got to that day off, I usually had to go to him. He didn't like driving his truck into Brooklyn. I'd get on the train and take it into Manhattan. Then I'd get on the bus and take it out to Jersey. When I finally arrived at his place, it seemed like he was always busy doing something else, even though he'd known I was coming. I'd walk in so excited to see him, and as soon as I saw that he was busy it just sort of put me on edge.

I'd say, "Hey. Um, hi. I'm here now. Let's hang out. Let's go do something."

And immediately, he'd be on edge, and he'd snap at me, "I can't just drop what I'm doing just because you finally showed up." It stung every time. I'd get tears in my eyes, and he'd roll his and add, "Oh, there you go, getting all emotional." Because he hated when I tried to manipulate him.

I said, through the tears that I couldn't stop from falling, "I thought you wanted to see me."

He'd say, "I did want to see you. I do. But I can't just change my entire schedule around yours."

"Well, if you want me to leave, I'll leave."

Usually, at this point, he'd soften. He'd say, "No. I'm not saying I want you to leave. It's just that you need to understand that we can't all do whatever Jessica wants us to do whenever she wants it."

I would stand there crying, not knowing if I should leave or if I should stay. Then he would get up and he'd come over to me and he'd start kissing me. And it was great. He was a great kisser. And then we'd have sex, and it was great too.

But my favorite part was always after. We would lay in bed together, and he would hold me. He was very tender. He'd lean over me and we'd stare into each other's eyes, and he would sing to me. He had the most beautiful voice. He didn't like my voice, so I couldn't sing with him, but I loved listening to him sing. Those moments when he would gaze into my eyes and sing to me were so lovely. They made me feel loved, desired, cared for. And I would think, "Yes, this is where I want to be. And I never want to leave."

Orpheus was the musician of the era. He was beloved by the people, the rulers, and the gods and goddesses of ancient Greece. He was so beloved that he could have whatever he wanted. He did have pretty much anything that he wanted, and yet one day, as he was walking through the woods, something caught his eye. He went to see what it was, and he beheld a lovely sight, a wood nymph, in all her naked beauty. It was her beauty that attracted him, but also the way she so tenderly cared for her trees. Orpheus knew that he wanted her for himself.

Eurydice saw Orpheus, and she thought that she wanted him too, at least for an afternoon. She did not intend to stay with him, to leave her home, her forest, behind. Orpheus, sensing that he might not have her for himself, did what he always did when he wanted something. He played his music for her. When the song ended and he held out his hand, Eurydice took it and Orpheus led her away.

Jake hated everything about the Northeast. He hated my job. He told me that they didn't treat me well, that they took advantage of me, of my subservient nature. He hated New York and Brooklyn and New Jersey. He was from Virginia. A Southern boy. He had grown up there, and he kept telling me over and over again that we would have a better life there. After two years of listening to him, I agreed. I agreed to leave my career and my friends and my family behind and move with him to Northern Virginia. We started looking for a house, and we found one just a couple of miles away from the house he grew up in, the house his parents still lived in. We'd be close to family, his family, and it was a house we could afford, sort of.

I had money. I had been working my whole life and had some savings. And I'd just gotten a settlement, so I could afford half of the down payment. Jake didn't have money. He came from money. His dad was a successful attorney, so Jake had pretty much just been given anything he needed, or wanted. And that's what happened now, sort of. Jake's dad agreed to loan us the other half of the deposit for the house. It was a loan, not a gift, but it allowed us to buy the house.

On the week we were supposed to be moving into our new house, Jake and his dad had a trip planned. They were supposed to go bear hunting in Canada.

I said, "Well, honey, I mean, we're moving into a new house together. This is kind of a huge step. I think your dad will understand if you need to cancel the trip."

Jake said, "You want me to cancel on my dad? My dad who just gave us the money to buy a house? I'm not going to do that. I'm not going to do that to him, and I expect you to be more understanding."

I didn't point out that his dad hadn't actually given us the money, that we had to pay it back. But I did understand his point. And I loved that he cared about his dad. That was a nice thing. I didn't want to be selfish and get in the way of that. I let him go on the trip.

The week before we were moving in, Jake packed up our stuff into a U-Haul, drove it down to Virginia, and left it in the driveway of our new, empty house. Then he headed to Canada with his dad, and I went out to New Jersey and picked up my mom. We drove down to Virginia together. Over the next week, she and I cleaned and unpacked and put stuff away and decorated and worked to make that house a home. It was a lot of work and a lot of decision-making, and I was kind of angry. I felt a little bit abandoned. But at the end of that week, when Jake came home, even though it was the middle of the night, he climbed into bed, into our bed, and he leaned over me, and he said, "I missed you so much. I'm so glad to be home." And I felt like I was ready to start my life with this man, in our home, and I never wanted to leave.

Eurydice was often alone in the palace. Orpheus continued to travel, to give performances, all over the empire. Eurydice missed her forest, too far away. She had trouble feeling at home in the palace. She did not make friends easily with the sophisticates of the city. Eurydice grew lonely. She sometimes felt abandoned and lost. Then Orpheus would return home, and he would play music for her, and they would make love. It was enough to sustain her for a little while longer, to keep her there until the next time.

Jake and I didn't stop fighting when we moved in together. Even though we lived in the same house, we didn't spend much time together. During the day, we worked apart. In the evening, we often ate in front of the TV, not talking. And when we were done with dinner, he'd go meet his friends. Usually, Jake's friends came to our house, so they'd meet in the basement or the game room. I would've played with them, hung out with them, but Jake was protective of his friendships. He guarded them, cherishing his time alone with his friends.

I grew a new life for myself. I made new friends, local friends, friends I liked. But still, I wanted to spend time with Jake. I would invite him to come to my writing group meetings. He'd always said he wanted to write more. But he didn't like my writing group. I invited him to play on my coed softball team, but he thought team sports were dumb. I tried to get him to come with me on trips home to NJ, to visit with my family or to attend family events, but he didn't like my family. When I tried to get him to spend time with my friends or family, he said, "It's not fair to expect me to spend time with them. You know I don't like them and I'll be miserable."

Truth be told, when I did manage to get him to come with me, to guilt or cajole him, he was so visibly annoyed the whole time that it wasn't worth it. He made me miserable on those occasions. I stopped asking him.

And then one day it occurred to me: I spent more time apart from Jake than with him. I said, "I'm tired of being alone in this relationship. We're already living separate lives. Maybe we should just think about going our separate ways."

While I was still considering how to make that separation happen, my birthday arrived and, with it, a gift from Jake. He gave me a six-week-old black Lab puppy. He put her in my arms, and she snuggled up to me and started licking my face, and I loved her right away. He said, "Now you won't be lonely anymore."

And as much as I had been determined to leave, it was no longer possible. I had a puppy, and she needed me.

Over time, Orpheus's trips became more and more extended. One day, after she'd been left alone for weeks, Eurydice decided that she would go and visit her forest. She hadn't been back in years. She'd longed to visit but never felt that she could go and return in time for Orpheus. But Orpheus was gone, and only the gods knew when he would be home again, and so she left.

Eurydice returned to her wood. When she arrived, she found that the trees no longer remembered her. They had grown hard and brittle from neglect. As she thought about it, she realized that she no longer remembered herself. She began to weep. Perhaps it was the tears that blinded her, or perhaps she chose not to see the snake that killed her.

When my puppy turned six months, we got her a brother. I had two times the dogs to care for, and two times the love, but still felt so alone. Nothing much else had changed about my relationship with Jake.

This one Friday night, Jake and his friends were having an epic gaming session. We had these computers networked together in our basement so that they could all play Diablo or Duke Nuke 'Em together. Sometimes I would play too. If there was room. But there was no computer for me this night, and I was feeling left out.

I tried to keep busy. I cleaned up, watched a little TV. But I wanted to be around people. I wanted to be with Jake. So, I went to the basement, and I just hung out in the room. Everyone else was playing together, and I was just sitting there by myself, probably trying to read. After a while, I got bored sitting there. I said, "Hey, guys. Do you think maybe we could play something else, like a game that I could play too?"

Jake's friends seemed okay with that idea, but Jake said, "What are you even doing here? You don't even like games."

Which stung. It wasn't true, first of all, and second of all I felt like he had just humiliated me in front of his friends. I got up and went upstairs to my bedroom. I wasn't thinking, really. I was just being emotional, crying. I started packing a bag. I didn't know where I was going to go, I just felt like I needed to leave.

Jake came upstairs, and in a tone you'd use for a child who was doing something wrong but also adorable, he said, "What are you doing?"

I said, "I'm going. I'm getting out of here. I need some space."

He said, "You're so emotional. Come on. You never play with us. Why would you want to play with us now?"

I said, "I feel like I never get to see you."

He said, "We see each other every day. We sleep together every night. How much more of me do you need?"

I said, "Do you even love me?"

He said, "Are you kidding? You are so selfish. You're sitting here accusing me of not loving you? You're sitting here thinking about leaving me? Do you know how much I love you? I love you so much that I have been spending the last few months shopping for a ring. Yeah, that's right. I bought you a ring. I'm planning to marry you. That's how much I love you. I'm going to spend the rest of my life with you, so you're going to get to see me all the time."

I was so shocked that he wanted to marry me that I didn't leave. A few weeks later, he proposed. It was really romantic and sweet. He took me to a fancy restaurant and was going to propose over dessert but was too nervous, so he did it in the parking lot after.

And then I had a wedding to plan, and that took a lot of my time. Our wedding was beautiful. Every detail was perfect. We danced our first dance to a song Jake had chosen, from his favorite band, Metallica. As we danced, he held me in his arms and I looked in his eyes, and he sang to me. I believed, with my whole heart, the words he sang. It was just him and me together, and nothing else mattered.

Orpheus learned of Eurydice's death and was dumbstruck. He could not imagine returning to his home, to his palace, to find that she was not waiting for him. He wanted her to be there when he returned to his home, as she was supposed to be. So he did what those who are beloved by the gods do. He went to them. He sought them out. He sought a boon. And because he was beloved by the gods, they granted him one. One chance to go down into Hades and bring Eurydice out and back to the land of the living. In exchange for a song. There was but one rule. No matter what, under no circumstances, could Orpheus, before stepping foot back in the land of the living, turn to look behind him.

The wedding was actually not as perfect as all that. It was complicated. A few weeks before the wedding, my mom got sick, and I was taking her to doctor's appointments while also trying to get everything done for the big day. A few days before our wedding, Mom was diagnosed with terminal cancer, and I was still trying to get everything done for the wedding, all by myself, because Jake wasn't helping.

After, I was trying to take care of my mom. I invited Mom to come and live with Jake and me full-time, since I was the only kid with a house and the one who was best set up to take care of her. But that pissed Jake off. "We just got married. We're newlyweds. We're trying to start our life together and you want your mother to come and live with us?!"

"She's dying. I'm the one who's taking her to chemotherapy and radiation. No one else can do that."

"Yeah, as usual. You're the only one in your family doing anything. And now I have to deal with it too."

Jake allowed Mom to move in, me to get a hospital bed installed, and for me to take time off of running my business to take care of my mom, but he wasn't happy about it.

Three months after the wedding, Mom was on her deathbed. I had taken her to my sister's apartment—about forty-five minutes away—a few days earlier. I was there with Mom, along with my sister and her boyfriend and my brother and his wife. We were all there at her deathbed, and nearby when she died. In the morning, after we'd made the funeral arrangements, after we'd made phone calls to family, after rush hour was over, I called Jake at work and told him the news.

He said the right things, that he was sorry for my loss and so on, and then I let him go back to work. I went back to grieving with my brother and his wife and my sister and her boyfriend. We spent the day together as a family, grieving the loss of our mother.

I went home that night, and it was nice to see the dogs again and to be at home again. Over dinner, Jake was joking with me. He said, "When I told my boss that your mom died, she was like, 'You should leave and take the rest of the week off to be with your wife,' 'cuz she doesn't understand our relationship. She doesn't understand that my wife isn't one of those needy women. My wife isn't so demanding."

And I felt proud. I was finally the kind of woman that Jake wanted me to be. Over the next year, I clung to that while I grieved my mother. I would not be needy. I threw myself into my work. I threw myself and the money I had inherited from my mom into the house, into redoing the kitchen, into making our house into that home I always wanted. I threw myself into taking care of our lovely, sweet, adoring dogs. I was self-sufficient. I didn't need anything from Jake.

And then this one day, something snapped in me. I was alone at home with the dogs, as I was so much of the time, and I just felt so lonely. I started crying about missing my mom. I missed having that person in my life who loved me unconditionally. As I was wiping the tears away, I found myself thinking, *I have to stop crying before Jake gets home. He doesn't like it when I get emotional.* And as soon as I had that thought, I immediately had another thought: *Who have I become? How have I turned into someone who is afraid to show emotion in front of the person who should care the most when I am emotional?*

Then I knew that I had to leave.

When he got home from work that night, I had decided. I was calm when I told him that I wanted a divorce.

He got angry, angry in a way I'd never seen him before. He said, "If you try to leave, I will take everything. And you know I can do it. You have nothing without me, no one. And my dad is a lawyer, so he will ruin you if you try to fight. I will take it all."

I knew it wasn't an idle threat. I knew I would lose everything if I left.

Orpheus descended into Hades and found Eurydice. He explained the rules to her, what he must and must not do to bring her home. Then he played a song, a beautiful song, that enchanted the entire realm and all of Earth, the heavens. When the song ended and Orpheus held out his hand to Eurydice, she took it. He led her toward the land of the living. But just as the opening to the surface was in sight, just as a return to life was directly before them, Orpheus felt a tug at his hand, and then nothing. Eurydice's hand was no longer in his. He called out to her. There was no answer. He sang out to her in his perfect, intoxicating voice. No voice answered back. He tried every way he could think of to elicit some response. There was naught but silence. Finally, he could wait no longer. He had to know. He could not continue any further without knowing if she was still there or if he had lost her forever. So he turned and looked back, whereby he beheld Eurydice walking away from him.

When I left, I walked away from the dogs I adored, the house that I had worked so hard to turn into a home, the money and time and effort I had put into the house, and all of the love that I had put into the past seven years of this relationship. I left it all behind. I walked forth, and I did not look back.

Chapter 14

I Said I Love You

I told my mom I love you all the time.

My mom came to stay with my fiancé, Jake, and me a few months before our wedding. She'd had health problems all of my life, so I was used to the medical situation, but everything seemed to be compounding. She needed to see lots of doctors and get a few minor surgeries, and it just seemed easier for her to come stay with us than for her to stay at home in New Jersey. I'd have to drive from Virginia to New Jersey to take her to doctors' appointments all the time. Plus, with a million things to get done before the wedding, it saved me time. Sort of. I didn't have to drive to New Jersey, but I did have to drive her around. And with all of the doctors' appointments and dress fittings, I had to catch up on all the work I was missing during the day when I'd get home. When you run your own business, you can make your own hours, but the work is unending. There never seemed to be any time to talk to my mom, even though she was staying with me. It felt like I didn't even see her.

I told my mom I love you all the time.

Two weeks before the wedding, my mom started having trouble breathing. She was afraid she was going to pass out, that she was going to suffocate. She couldn't get the air into her lungs. I called 911. While we were waiting for the ambulance to arrive, my phone rang. It was a woman from the wedding venue. She said that they needed the final payment, that it was two weeks before the wedding date. I explained how we were waiting for an ambulance and my mom was sick and she was going to be going to the hospital, but she said that they wouldn't wait, that if I didn't pay them right then they were going to cancel our reservation. I had to put her on hold to go open the door for the EMTs, and while the EMTs were taking care of my mom, I got out my purse and my credit card. I got back on the phone with the wedding venue woman, and I gave her all of the information that she needed to secure our wedding. By the time I got off the phone, the EMTs were loading my mom into an ambulance to take her to the hospital.

I told my mom I love you all the time.

Mom only spent one night in the hospital. She had so many health problems that the doctors didn't really tell us anything new other than that she needed to have more tests done, see more doctors. Three days before the wedding, my mom had a follow-up appointment at an oncologist's office. Mom had gone to stay with my sister at this point because I had so much to get done before the wedding, plus some of the groomsmen were from out of town and they were staying at our house. I was still trying to finish up all the work I needed to get done before taking off for a wedding and a honeymoon—sending out invoices, making sure my clients were informed I'd be away, and giving them the number for my subcontractor in case they did need any work done in my absence. Plus, I needed to get everything done for the wedding. But I still made time to meet my mom and my sister at the oncologist's office. I'd never heard anyone say "You have three months to one year left to live" before, so I was completely unprepared. My mom and my sister and I hugged and sobbed until there was nothing left in our bodies to give, and then we went and got pizza.

I told my mom I love you all the time.

When I got home from the oncologist, and the pizza, Jake came out to meet me in the driveway. I told him the prognosis. I told him my mom was going to die. The whole conversation took maybe three minutes. His friends were in from out of town, and there were three days left until the wedding. He had a lot of gaming he had to fit into those three days. He didn't really have time to talk. I didn't have time either. I was making the party favors and the place cards and the seating charts and the centerpieces, so I just got right back to work on everything that needed to get done. A few hours later, one of the groomsmen, this guy Colby, whom I knew a little but hadn't spent much time with, came out of the game room and sat down with me. Jake had told him the news. I knew that Colby's mom had died a few years earlier from cancer. Colby said, "You're probably not ready to hear this. I know I wasn't ready to hear it. But I need to say it. Death is surprisingly final. You can't get your mom back. After my mom died, there were a million questions I wished I had asked her. Ask your mom anything, any questions that you have for her, now. Talk to her as much as possible and tell her you love her like you mean it, because you won't get another chance." Colby got up and went back to the game room, and I got back to work on the wedding. There were a million things to do, and besides . . .

I told my mom I love you all the time.

After the honeymoon, I took over as my mom's full-time caregiver. She officially moved in with me, and we packed up and sold her house. I spent my days going to doctors' appointments with her, picking up medical supplies and medicine, and taking her to radiation—palliative radiation—five days a week. When we got back from all of our errands, from running around like crazy, I would get back to work, trying to catch up on the emails and editing and invoices and scheduling and everything I was missing. There was never time to talk. There was never time for anything. By the end of the day, I was exhausted from working myself to the bone, and my mom was exhausted from the cancer. So, we would sit on the couch and zone out in front of the TV until one of us had to go to bed. Then we'd say good night and "I love you." And that was another day gone.

I told my mom I love you all the time.

Three months to the day after our wedding, my mom lay on her deathbed in a fever dream brought on by cancer and morphine. There was no way to ask her any questions at this point. There was no way she could talk at this point. So, I told her all the things you're supposed to say to someone whom you love, to someone who is dying. I said that we would be okay. I said that she could let go, that she could move on to a better place. And I told her that I loved her. I don't know if she heard me at that point but . . .

I told my mom I love you all the time. I just hope she knew that I meant it.

Chapter 15

Life's a Marathon

My parents told me I could do anything if I just set my mind to it. And you know what? That worked. If I set my mind to it, I could read a million books, learn French, excel at art. These were, of course, intellectual pursuits, and I was good at those.

Physical pursuits, not so much. I dropped out of soccer, track, and field hockey. My family all called me a quitter, but I preferred quitting to sticking with things I hated, like practice, ugh. By the time I finished high school, I was happy setting my mind on more cerebral things.

And that served me pretty well until 2006, when my sister, Heather, called me and said, "I have a great idea."

Normally, when my sister says she has a great idea, that's a good time to save myself some trouble by hanging up the phone. But I was going through a divorce and feeling extra lonely. I was all ears.

"Let's sign up to run the Phoenix marathon together!"

"Uh, no. I don't like running a mile. Why would I ever run more than that?"

"We can hang out every weekend while we run, and last time

I did a marathon my ass looked amazing!" She added, knowing my weakness, "And it's a great way to meet guys."

Being newly single, I needed to get in shape, and where could I meet more guys than in training for a huge race?

I met my sister at our first training run only to find out it was 90 percent chicks. If I had thought about it for two seconds, I would have realized men don't need help training for a marathon—just like they don't need help with directions.

I was a little unhappy at the start of the day, but about ten hours later, after I got through my first three-mile run, I felt kind of cool. It was 9:00 a.m. on a Saturday, and I had already run three miles.

I was feeling pretty good about this whole marathon training decision until the day before the next weekend's run, when my sister called again. "I am sorry. Don't kill me. I can't train for a marathon right now."

To tell you the truth, I wasn't surprised. What surprised me more was my response.

"Okay, fine, drop out, but I am still doing it." I think it was partly out of spite—like see what you made me do—but also, I had done my three runs that week, and I definitely was not enjoying them, but I was enjoying having done them.

Running sucks, but what I figured out is that distance running is all mental. It's not about what your body is doing. It's about what your mind is doing. I came to think of training like going to work. I had no choice. I had to go, do my time, and get the job done. And once I framed it that way, I just did it.

That's how I got through my first ten-mile run and then twelve and then sixteen. I had to do it, so I did. And even though I didn't meet boys, I made some great friends.

I ran most weekends with my friends Erika and Deb. Erika was usually a lot of fun. But on our eighteen-mile run, she changed. She got mean, snippy, and annoyed with everything. It was kind of fun to watch, actually—like being sober when one of your friends is wasted. But she wasn't wasted; she had hit the wall.

The coaches trained us up to twenty miles before the race. I was fully expecting to have the worst brought out in me on the twenty-mile run, which was in late February, but the night before, nature, instead, brought out her worst.

That morning, everything was covered in ice. This was our last chance to train twenty miles before the marathon, so I met Erika and Deb out on the trail.

It turns out that running twenty miles on ice is easier than running twenty miles on road —because you can't run. The best we managed was maybe an occasional jog, but for the most part we spent that day doing the penguin. It took seven hours, but none of us hit any kind of wall.

A few weeks later, we flew to Phoenix for the race. And here's the thing: it's warm there in March. It was in the high seventies with zero percent humidity. It was so great to be out of winter. The morning of the race, I didn't have to wear a garbage bag to stay warm or anything.

Now, being fairly slow, I was corralled, with Erika and Deb, pretty far back in line. It took a good thirty minutes after the gun fired the start of the race before we got to cross the start line, but that was a great moment. I was running a marathon.

We were going along at a healthy clip. The marathon route has big digital signs announcing each mile. Mile one passed. Mile two. I was feeling good. For someone who had quit track after realizing that one mile was a long way to go, just being in this race felt like an accomplishment.

And then I face-planted. Somewhere around mile three, I tripped.

I was more stunned than hurt. My knee was scraped up, so I just lay there, not knowing what to do. And no, people don't stop. Even though we were way back with the people who had no chance of winning, they jumped over me or shot me dirty looks as they ran around me.

That's when Erika took off, and I thought *Wow, I made it to three miles before failing.* But Deb gave me hand sanitizer and a Band-And, and it was obvious she was waiting for me. So I got up, and we continued running.

I was fine. A little embarrassed, but my knee didn't hurt and we had hardly lost any time. In fact, we could see Erika in front of us for most of the race.

The next ten or so miles went by without anything exciting happening. It's hard to believe, but when you have trained for five months, running thirteen miles is not a big deal.

But somewhere around fourteen miles in, I started to feel crappy. I knew Deb was a little slower than I was at my natural gait, and I got the idea that if I ran more at my pace, I would feel better.

I said goodbye and took off, but it didn't help. I was feeling worse and worse—crampy, weak. It didn't seem to matter how much Gatorade I drank; I was so thirsty, something I wasn't used to from running in the cold. Then I noticed the salt deposits on my arms. Piles of them had built up, and I remembered that we weren't in winter anymore.

I put two and two together—dizziness, fatigue, cramps, salty arms in warm weather. I was losing too much salt. I stopped at a first aid tent, grabbed a few salt packets, washed one down, and walked it off until I felt better. After that, I took salt regularly and didn't cramp up again.

I got back in the race. I ran past the sixteen-mile marker, the eighteen, the twenty. I even made it to twenty-one miles, the farthest I had ever gone, and that's when my mind betrayed me. I felt angry. This was the dumbest thing I had ever done. Why was I here? This was miserable and now I was stuck and why was it so freaking hard to move?! I felt like I was trying to jog but getting nowhere. Like every step was trying to push through a giant wall of Jell-O.

When you are feeling good, you don't notice that you are being passed by moms pushing baby carriages and couples wearing parrot costumes, but when you've hit the wall, that shit gets annoying. If

I had had more energy, I would've started punching people. You think it's cute to wear a funny costume and run a marathon? What, a marathon's like a joke to you? Oh, I was done with the whole thing.

My running slowed to a jog, then to a walk, and then really just to an upright crawl. Every step was torture, and that pissed me off more, because I didn't want to keep moving, but I couldn't stop.

My only option, other than going forward, was to quit. But quitting meant sitting in a tent until the race was over and a van would take me to the finish line. Even at the pace I was going, I would be done with the misery of this stupid race well before then.

I kept moving—one foot in front of the other. I kept thinking. A marathon is twenty-six miles because some Greek soldier ran that distance to Athens and then he died. Yeah, thanks a lot, buddy. And to make it worse, the English tacked on 0.2 miles for some Royals back in the day. And I gotta tell ya, the twenty-six-mile marker feels an awful lot like the end of the race, but it's not.

No. Thanks to some ancient English people, you get to keep going. I did not want to keep going. But even though I was covered in salt, limping like a zombie and feeling like death, when I rounded that last corner, with maybe 0.1 miles to go, there were a million people cheering, and I felt like I had to at least try to run over the finish line. It wasn't pretty, but I did it.

And as soon as I crossed the finish line, the pain was forgotten. I was so happy, I was crying. Partly to be done, yes, but also because I just felt so good about myself. I hadn't quit. I had finished a marathon.

And when it was over, the one thought that kept going through my mind, and the one belief that was cemented for me during that run and is still with me today, is that I can do anything if I just put my mind to it.

Chapter 16

The Game

I was thirty-three years old, recently divorced, and the new owner of a small townhouse and an even smaller business when I went out, looking for love. I went to a meetup for singles. It was being hosted by someone I knew through business networking. It was my first and last singles night. It was at a hotel bar, and when I walked into the event, I was pretty disappointed by what I saw. All the guys seemed way older than me, way more out of shape, and lacking any kind of style. In other words, it looked just like a business networking event.

I grabbed a glass of wine and stood at a table, trying to figure out how long I needed to stay to not insult the host. And then, I saw it—across the room—a beacon of hope. A guy standing there who was not Brad Pitt or Hugh Jackman, but he would do. He was wearing clothes made post-1970, could still see his toes past his belly, and wouldn't remember where he was the day Kennedy was shot.

I caught his eye and waited. A few minutes later, he was at my table making small talk and asking for my number.

Roy and I had our first date over burgers. The fact that I ordered a burger instead of a salad or something seemed like a ploy to him—like I was playing at not caring about what I was eating on a first date. But I don't play games. I just happen to love a good burger.

As the night wrapped up, he asked me to guess how old he was, which was awkward. I am terrible with ages, and I didn't want to insult him. He looked like he was in his forties, but I figured it would be safer to guess way below that, so I said thirty-five. He laughed and said no, really? So I said thirty-nine? We played the guessing game a little longer, but he said he'd only give me the answer on our next date.

There was nothing wrong with our first date. I wasn't blown away, but I had fun, and he had fun, so we met for the second date. I got to learn how old he was—not yet thirty. It's not my fault he looked like a well-preserved forty-year-old instead of a not-so-in-shape twenty something! We laughed about it and moved on, and he was convinced I had just been playing him.

Six months later, we were still dating, just dating. It was fun. He was nice, made good money, made me laugh. He was a good catch. Whenever we hung out with my family, my nieces called him Uncle Roy and he made them laugh and was great with them, and then my belly started making this ticking noise, and I remembered that I was over thirty.

I said, "We should be exclusive, or we should break up."

He said, "I like my freedom."

I said, "You never date anyone else. I'm the only one dating other people."

He said, "I just want to keep my options open."

It was infuriating. I was the one with options, not him, but he didn't want to commit. I didn't have time to waste, so I said, "Fine, let's break up." He thought I was joking, but I don't play games. He didn't want to break up, so we stopped seeing other people.

There was nothing wrong with our relationship. We never fought. We had the same sense of humor. We got along great. Neither of us demanded much of the other, and I always had a date for the weekend. It wasn't fireworks and romance, but I was thirty-three and ready to settle for grown-up love. And then it was six months later and my belly was still ticking, even if my heart wasn't exactly pounding.

I made him laugh, put up with his crappy hours at work, and cooked him a lot of great meals. It bugged me that he wasn't pushing for more of a commitment. I am a great catch. Hello!

"We should move in together."

He said, "I don't think I am ready."

I said, "Well maybe we should break up then."

He said, "You wouldn't leave me. You love me too much."

But I wasn't playing. I said "Fine, let's break up," so he said, "No, no, let's move in together." And that's when things changed.

It was like those scenes in *Bugs Bunny* where Bugs is arguing with Elmer Fudd. Elmer says get in the cauldron. Bugs says no. Elmer says yes. Bugs say no. Elmer says yes. Bugs says yes, and then Elmer's saying no and Bugs is saying yes and it's all flipped around.

As soon as Roy said, "Okay, let's move in together," I thought, "Oh shit, I don't want that." And then I was saying "No, no. We should take our time and think about it," but he had outplayed me.

"You can live with me and rent out your townhouse," he said. He was ready to do it. And there I was with this ticking belly but no pounding heart.

It was my move. I said, "I think we really should break up."

He still thought it was a game. He said, "Are you trying to protect me? Are you dying and don't want me to know?"

I said, "No. I am not."

He said, "Where did this come from? Are you having a nervous breakdown?"

I said, "No, I'm not. I am sorry."

He came by a few days later to return my stuff. He asked me if we could go for a walk. We were in the woods behind my house when he said, "You win." He held out a diamond ring and said, "I am in love with you. I am sorry I made you wait, but I want to spend the rest of my life with you."

My heart stopped. This wasn't what I had wanted. I said, "I can't marry you. I don't love you." At first, he thought I was playing games. He promised me a bigger ring, a better proposal at a future date. I had to convince him that I meant it, and when I did, he told me I was crazy, and he meant it, and then we did break up, for real.

He had thought all along that I was playing him. I realized I had been. I had been playing at making him love me, because I thought he should. And in the end, I won.

Chapter 17

I'd Buy That for a Dollar

I found my husband on the internet, specifically MySpace.

I was training for my first marathon with TNT, Team in Training. When you train with TNT, you also have to fundraise, thousands of dollars. TNT volunteers train you for the race, you raise money—and also run a marathon—to support the Leukemia & Lymphoma Society. I was actually more nervous about raising the money than running the marathon. I mean, I was recently divorced and paying for everything by myself. I couldn't just write a check for $3,000. I had to actually raise the money, and I sadly did not have any rich friends who could write me a check.

My friend Meredith worked in fundraising, and she suggested I throw a bachelor/bachelorette auction – where we would auction off dates with singles. The only problem was that Meredith – who helped pull the whole event together - and I were both single women. We knew plenty of other single women, but no single guys. If we were going to auction off dates with anyone male, we were going to need to find some.

This was back in the days of MySpace, and I gotta tell ya, I miss those days. It was such a great platform. One of the benefits was that you could search for friends on MySpace by location and by other parameters, like gender and relationship status. I put in "single men in a 50-mile radius" and got a nice list to work from.

I was selflessly raising money to cure cancer, after all, so I didn't feel too bad writing to strange men and asking them if they'd go on a date for charity. And if I enjoyed perusing the choices, is that wrong?

I probably wrote to fifteen guys and did end up having six to auction off. But there was only one guy whom I actually felt selfish about. I told Meredith that if he went to auction, I was going to bid on him because he, well, I don't know how to say this without sounding shallow, but he was fine. Yummy, even. Gorgeous blue eyes. A perfect five-o'clock shadow. And great lighting on his cowboy-hat-wearing self-portrait. I mean, that was the hook. Then I read his profile.

He was a smart, funny, athletic nerd. In other words, a unicorn. My perfect guy, on paper at least.

I was more nervous about asking him to the auction than I had been with any of the others. Because there was something at stake with him. I wanted him to say yes. I wanted to go on a date with him.

He did respond to my message. Which was good. But his response was "No, absolutely not." And then, as if to soften the harshness of the negative response, he added, "See my number one fear."

Back in the day, MySpace had fun little sections like "Favorite quote," "Music you love," and "Fears." His only fear was public speaking. OMG. He was superhot, smart, athletic, funny, AND shy? Now I really wanted to meet him.

Here's the other thing—I ran a video company, and he was a graphic artist and 3D animator. In other words, I had another in.

I wrote saying that I was sorry he couldn't help me raise money, because I was sure he would've raised a lot—for the cause. And then I said, "Do you ever do freelance work? We could meet for a coffee and discuss ways to work together."

In retrospect, that was a little slimy, but since he said no and we never got to take it to inappropriate-coffee-meeting levels, I'm gonna pretend that my motives were noble.

He was busy enough and didn't need any freelance work, but we did start a conversation about work, about navigating the treacherous waters of trying to deliver creative work to business clients. There are many things to unpack on that subject, and the conversation, in MySpace messenger, went on for weeks, with some side conversations about movies and other fun stuff too. Never anything too personal.

I raised all the money I needed to raise and more and ran my first marathon without embarrassing myself too much. I had recently moved into my townhouse, and after all the marathon stuff settled down, I hosted a housewarming party. I invited my new marathon running friends and I invited Mark. He RSVP'd yes. I was so excited to meet him face-to-face. I was still single—I hadn't bid on anyone at that auction after all—and still holding a little torch for this guy who looked great on paper and who was fun to chat with online.

Let me take a moment to set the stage for those who are younger and wiser. Back in my day, internet dating was new. That meant that not everyone had done it. It also meant that not everyone had gotten wise to the fact that on dating sites, people didn't always use their real photos or current photos or untouched-up photos. And Facebook wasn't widespread yet, so most people's profile pictures were just photos they had taken while out having fun with friends and family, not carefully curated pictures from a long line of selfies, each set up and taken at the perfect angle to hide all your flaws. In other words, I expected Mark to look as good as his MySpace profile picture.

And he did. When he walked into my townhouse, it was like a scene from a movie. The crowd went quiet. They parted for him, and I swear a spotlight followed him as he walked into my kitchen and put down the Moose Munch he'd brought. He had on a leather jacket. I learned later that it was a motorcycle jacket. (OMG!) His hair was black, but already streaked with a little gray. And his eyes were so blue and piercing, like a predator hunting for prey. If he'd had a British accent, and no fear of public speaking, he could've played a great movie villain.

We said hi to each other, and I introduced him to some of my friends, and then he moved off one way and I another. He was at the party for only an hour or two, but every time I looked over at him, we locked eyes across the room and I'd end up blushing. After he left—after a very tame, bodies-nowhere-near-each-other hug goodbye—several friends came up to me to tell me he was watching me the whole night, that he was looking at me like he wanted to devour me. I was sure there'd be more fun soon.

But a few days later, his relationship status changed to "in a relationship," and I had to let it go.

A year and a half went by. I started dating Roy somewhere in there. I got a roommate to help with the cost of the townhouse. Mark and I stayed in touch, a little here and there. I'd tell him about a movie I saw; he'd tell me about a bike race he rode in. We migrated our relationship to Facebook.

I signed up to run two marathons in one season, with TNT. First, I'd go to San Francisco to run the Nike Women's Marathon and then back to DC a week later for the Marine Corps. There was more money to fundraise. Meredith helped me set up another bachelor/bachelorette auction. I didn't put myself in it this time, and I didn't ask Mark. We were both in relationships.

A few weeks before the San Francisco marathon, Mark's relationship status changed to "it's complicated." I sent him a funny video and checked in to see how he was doing. In the meantime, I began the long process of breaking up with Roy. Mark potentially being single might've helped motivate my choice to break up with Roy—but I was well aware that there was no guarantee anything would happen with Mark.

The Nike Women's Marathon in San Francisco was wonderful. I broke up with Roy before flying out there, ran a great race, hung out with friends, and sent Mark a couple texts—we had exchanged phone numbers recently—from California. After I got back to Virginia, I had less than a week before the DC marathon. I broke up with Roy, again, as it hadn't quite taken yet.

The night before the DC marathon was also the night before Mark's annual wiener roast and tramp party. He had a trampoline in his backyard, and a firepit. (Yes, the dream just keeps getting better!) I was invited to the party, but as it was a few hours after I was running a marathon. I didn't know if I would make it. I RSVP'd "maybe."

By then, Mark's relationship status was officially single, and as far as I was concerned, so was mine. The night before the marathon was the only night Mark and I both had free since this miracle of us both being officially single at the same time had finally happened. I still didn't know if anything was going to happen with Mark, but I really wanted it to. I invited him to my house for a movie night, telling him it had to end early because I had to get up at 5:00 a.m. for the marathon.

We sat chastely on my couch and watched a cheesy fantasy movie. I couldn't concentrate anyway. I was so aware of Mark just inches away from me. I could hear him breathing, wondered if he could hear me breathing. And was it too loud? Was I mouth breathing? Did my stomach make a noise? I couldn't eat the popcorn he brought because that would definitely be too loud.

The movie was awful, but so was sitting there for ninety minutes staring at a screen and trying not to breathe too much. And then it was close to 10:00 p.m. and I had to go to sleep.

Mark very graciously got up and put on his motorcycle jacket to leave, saying he knew I had to get up early.

But nothing had happened! We were alone together, both now single, and I thought we were into each other—but he was leaving!

He had parked his motorcycle out on the street beyond the cul-de-sac that my townhouse community sat on. I offered to walk him to his motorcycle. He laughed at that but allowed me to take his arm as we walked out to the street together.

I gave him a weak hug at his bike and turned to go back to my house. He started walking back with me.

I said, "What are you doing?"

He said, "Walking you to your door."

I laughed at that but allowed him to take my arm as he walked me to my front step. There I gave him a real hug, bodies pressed together, arms wrapped around each other. Neither of us seemed to want to let go. I started to pull away, slowly, our cheeks pressing together. As our lips passed near each other, we started kissing. Finally!

It was amazing. Such a great kiss. And it went on for forever. Like hours. To the point where it was too late for me to let him drive his motorcycle home. And it was also late for me to be getting to bed before a marathon.

I said, "You can sleep in my room, but we are keeping our clothes on and going right to bed, because I have to get up in a few hours."

He totally agreed. And that's just what we did. No nooky nor nothing. I can't say I slept at all. If sitting beside him on the couch with a movie playing had been tough, lying beside him in my bed was way harder! He could definitely hear me breathing. And I definitely could not fall asleep.

It was both endless and too short of a night before my alarm went off and I had to kick him out, get dressed, and drag myself downtown to the start of the race. I said goodbye to Mark and promised to try to make it to his wiener roast. I wasn't really sure where we stood after one night together. I knew I had fun and wanted more. Like I wanted him back. I didn't want to go run a marathon at all at this point. But tired as I was, I wasn't about to miss the marathon.

So, I went and ran a marathon. It was awful. I was so fatigued and in so much physical pain from not having eaten properly or rested properly that every step after maybe mile five was just torture. And my stomach hurt. I'd never had stomach problems running before.

Apparently, all those times I'd properly prepared to run marathons in the past had worked to keep the cramps away. Staying up all night, hardly eating, and not properly hydrating was definitely not good pre-race prep. I was feeling awful.

But right at about mile marker sixteen, I saw someone. It was Mark. He was just standing there waving. And I couldn't help myself. I ran up to him and gave him a kiss, and it felt so right. He kissed me back, despite my sweat and the whole mess I was in. And I ran on, buoyed by the fact that I had a wiener roast to get to.

After I got home and showered, I headed over to Mark's house for his party. It was when I arrived at the gate to his backyard that I was hit with this moment of doubt. I didn't know anyone who was going. I didn't know where I stood with Mark. We had one make-out session. We were both newly single. He was having a party and had invited me, along with a whole bunch of other people. What was I walking into? What was our status?

I stepped into his backyard, and a guy came up to me and offered to take the beer I'd brought to put it in the cooler. Someone else pointed out where the firepit was. I tried to not seem awkward or uncomfortable as I met his friends, wondering where he was, where we stood, what would happen when he saw I was there.

It was a few minutes after I arrived that he walked up to me by the fire. I held my breath, letting him make the first move. These were his friends, his fire, his party.

He walked up to me, kissed me on the lips, took my hand, and didn't let go of it for the rest of the night.

That was the last time I was ever unsure of where I stood with him. We were practically inseparable after that—other than going to work. We fell so easily in love with each other that he and I were saying "I love you" daily within weeks of that first kiss. We were planning marriage and moving in together and kids within months.

Kind of like training for and properly preparing to run a marathon—it was a long road to get to him, but worth the time in the end.

Chapter 18

There's Always One

I started my own video production company over twenty years ago. At the time, I was one of the few women that I saw—women videographers and women bosses. They were out there; I just didn't see a lot of us. But over the years that began to change. I was getting hired by more women. I was working with more women.

Then, about fifteen years ago, I started working with construction companies. They have become regular clients. When a new building is nearing completion, they need to videotape training on the equipment in the building. The trainings go on for two to six months, so I end up getting a lot of long-term work from construction companies. Of course, when I started working with them, I was the only woman around. I didn't see any other women anywhere on the job. But again, over the years that has started to change.

Last year, I got hired by a new construction client, and the woman who hired me, Sarah, was the project manager on the site. On the first day, I went to meet Sarah and the guys, because everyone else was a man. I arrived on the jobsite with my PPE—my hard hat and vest—on. I had my video camera mounted on my tripod, set up and ready to videotape training. I said hi to Sarah and then to everyone else. There were twelve men—two of the guys leading the training and the rest there to be trained. And it was fine. The introductions went smoothly, until I got to the last guy. He said, "What is that, 4K?"

He was talking about my camera, because it's a high-resolution camera. It was just the way he said it. I could tell he was gonna be trouble. So, I deflected with humor, as I often do. I said, "Yeah, but I don't shoot these trainings in 4k because no one wants to see you guys close up."

Everybody laughed, and I thought, *Good, we've moved on.* But no. He kept going. He said, "Can I borrow it?"

I said, "No. This is an expensive camera, and I need it for work. You can't borrow it." Trying to just shut this down.

But he kept going, adding, "Because, you know, the wife and me can make some good videos with that. I mean some really good videos. You know, like, in the bedroom."

Why? Why did he have to go there? This is my first time meeting these people I have to work with for months. I got so uncomfortable, and I didn't want to deflect with humor because I didn't want to encourage him. And I didn't want to be mean because I've gotta work with him, so I didn't know what to do. Lacking any other good ideas, I just turned my back to him. When I did, I met Sarah's gaze. She rolled her eyes and said, "There is always one."

After college, I worked in the film industry, and after a few years of that, I decided I'd go work for a corporate video production company. I sent out my résumé to hundreds of video production companies in the Tristate Region, and then I waited. For months, I heard nothing. I was applying to work at corporate video production companies. I thought they would want to snatch me up. I had graduated with honors from NYU, one of the best film schools in the country. I'd gone to work in the feature film industry in New York, working with respected directors like Jim Jarmusch, and one of the movies I had worked on won an Academy Award—not because of me, but my name is in the credits just the same. I thought all these corporate video companies would love to hire me, if for no other reason than to put my résumé on their website. But no. I didn't hear from anyone for months.

Then, finally, this guy Bob called me up and invited me to come work for him for a trial period. I needed the money and I needed the job, so I said yes. I showed up on Monday to Bob's place. Bob worked out of his home in NJ. He lived on the third floor. On the second floor was the editing suite, and on the first floor was the reception area and the kitchen.

Bob was about sixty-five. Retired military. The editor who worked on the second floor was about thirty-five, also retired military. The only other person who worked there was this older woman who was the receptionist. After Bob gave me the grand tour, he led me into his office, which was on the first floor, to give me my orientation. The first thing he said to me was "You know, we all make the coffee here. If I ask you to make the coffee, it's not because you're a woman."

I've made a lot of coffee. It's fine. Bob continued, "Sometimes you will have to answer the phone. Let me see you do it."

I don't know if it was the fact that he made me pretend to answer the phone over and over and over again or the fact that he gave me directions like "Louder. Smile when you answer the phone. I want to see you smile." Or that he watched me so closely as I did it. The whole experience of performing for him made me feel like I was on the casting couch.

When that was done, I was free to go about my day, which involved mostly running errands, printing up labels, and labeling VHS tapes. And that's how the rest of the week went. Every day,

I did menial tasks, and every day I was called into Bob's office for uncomfortable conversations. One day, he wanted to share with me that he and the editor did drugs. Another day, he told me that this one time, for Halloween, he and the editor had dressed up as women. He'd say this stuff and then watch me, like he was trying to shock me. I didn't react, partly because I didn't want to give him the satisfaction and partly because I had just come from living in the East Village and working in the film industry. I had seen it all, and more.

On Friday of that first week, Bob took me to a room I'd never been to on the second floor. It was an editing suite. Well, it was a closet, but there was an editing system, of a sort, in there. The deck was old and unfamiliar. It certainly predated even the equipment in my high school video production classes. It was an A/B-roll kind of deck-to-deck editing system. Bob asked, "Can you use this?"

I said, "I can try."

Then he sat me down in front of the monitor, and he sat next to me. It was such a small room that our knees were touching. He told me he wanted me to edit his vacation video. Then he watched me while I watched the monitor. He told me what I was seeing. He'd gone on vacation recently in Sweden, and this was footage of an outdoor art exhibition about control. What I was seeing on the monitor was a naked guy walking another naked guy on a dog leash. As Bob watched me for a reaction that I refused to give him, I thought, *Yeah. This is about control.*

On Monday morning, Bob called and told me I didn't need to come in. My trial period had passed and I had failed. Even though I needed the money, I have never been so relieved to have been fired from a job.

A few hours later, another guy, from a different video production company in New Jersey, called me and asked if I could start that week. I said yes.

I started working for Dan two days later. His office was one large room, with a glass wall and door, in an office suite. Dan sat at his desk and made phone calls, and I sat at my desk and edited videos on a real editing system. On my first day, while I was already at work editing actual work footage, Dan was sitting at his desk looking at me. I looked up from my monitor and said, "What?"

He said, "You know, my friends—the other guys who also own video companies in the area—they think I'm crazy for hiring a woman."

I said, "Yeah? Why's that?"

He said, "Well, they all think that I'm going to get sued for sexual harassment."

I said, "Well, don't give me a reason and I won't sue you."

I worked for Dan for two years, and he never gave me a reason. I worked for Bob for one week and he gave me a million reasons, and yet it never occurred to me to sue him. In fact, it had never even occurred to me that anything about his behavior was shocking.

After I stopped working for Dan, I moved to Virginia and started my own video production company. Being a woman business owner has all the same challenges as being a male business owner. You've got to find clients, do good work, get paid, and repeat. But there's sometimes this added layer as a woman where it's not always clear what the mostly men who are hiring you really want from you. For example, this one marketing guy hired me to cover an expo—shoot some B-roll footage and edit it together into a sizzle reel, to show how awesome the event was. Rather than give me—the professional videographer he had hired—a shot list to work from, he went with me to the expo and followed close behind me the whole time, watching the monitor over my shoulder as I set up each shot. And it was never exactly what he wanted. So, he had to put his hands on my waist and pull me this way or put his arm around my shoulder and hold me just enough so that he could get exactly what he wanted.

Then there was Jeff. I met Jeff at a networking event, a business mixer. He was maybe sixty years old, dressed in a suit. I was thirty-four or so, also in a suit. He told me what he did—he was a contractor—and I told him what I did. He was excited when he heard. He said, "I'm so glad I met you. One of my clients has this big installation happening tomorrow in New Jersey, and I haven't found anyone to videotape it. Do you happen to have someone who could cover it?"

I said, "Well, I actually do know someone in New Jersey." I called up Dan, and he was able to go and videotape the installation. I got the footage from him, and I edited it into a promo for Jeff's clients and then sent it off to Jeff for approval. He was happy, his clients were happy, and they paid me, so I was happy, and the job was done.

About a week later, Jeff called and said, "It was great working with you. Why don't we get together for lunch? We could talk about some more ways we might be able to work together."

I said yes. We do this all the time in business. It's called networking. I went out to lunch with Jeff. It was good. He told me about his history of work and what he did for his clients, and I told him about my background and what I did for my clients. At the end, he offered to pay the bill and I said, "No. You're my client. I got it." And lunch was over.

I moved on with my week as normal, except that that Friday, Jeff called me, just to talk. It was a little bit out of the blue, especially since we'd just seen each other. And he didn't have any new clients to refer or any new work to discuss. But I didn't want to be rude, so I chatted with him.

It was going fine. And then he told me what he was going to do that weekend and asked me what I was going to do. I said, "My boyfriend and I are going away for the weekend."

There was silence, before the bomb exploded. He snapped, "You have a boyfriend? I suppose you were never going to tell me that, huh? You just like to lead guys on so you can get work from them! You know what that makes you?"

I won't repeat what he called me. Being a woman boss has some added challenges. Sometimes, when a man hires me, he thinks it's for more than just video production.

On the construction site, after the guy asked to borrow my camera to make a video with his wife, I looked at Sarah and she rolled her eyes and said, "There is always one."

I couldn't help but think back over the many more than one I have dealt with in the past twenty years alone. But then, looking at Sarah, I thought, *She might be the only other woman in the room, but she is also the one who is managing this job and writing my checks. And that gives me hope.*

I have hope that one day, maybe even soon, "there's always one" will be referring to the one guy who's about to get reprimanded, or fired, for his inappropriate or inexcusable behavior. Or maybe it will mean that there's always one woman boss in the room, hiring another woman boss. Maybe even one day, not too far away, when there are as many women, and women bosses, in the room as men, there won't be any reason left for any of us to say "there is always one."

Chapter 19

Surprise Ending

As a cinephile, avid reader, writer, epic planner, and storyteller, I am really hard to surprise. I can guess where most plots are going, and I can guess if someone I know is planning something. Of course, I love surprises. I crave surprises. But I almost never get surprised.

When my now husband Mark and I decided we would get married, it was early May. We wanted to do it that same year and not wait. But just because we'd decided to marry didn't mean we were officially engaged, and Mark really wanted to propose to me before we started doing the wedding planning.

I am the planner in the family. Mark, on the other hand, is more of a see-where-the-day-takes-you kinda guy. Not only did I have to wait for him to plan an engagement before I could plan our wedding, but I also had absolutely no hope of it being a surprise.

I already felt like I didn't have enough time, and as May flew by, I got more and more anxious and couldn't help but obsess about when he was going to do it already.

I figured he would most likely pop the question on a special occasion or a holiday. My birthday is in June, and when it arrived you know I opened every present carefully, searching for any stray diamond rings, but it wasn't a birthday proposal.

June came and went with no engagement, and I was like a caged beast waiting to get out there and plan this wedding but needing Mark to let me at it.

Fortunately, Fourth of July weekend looked promising. We were going to his folk's lake house in NC. The fireworks were Saturday night, over the lake, and Mark's folks were gone that day, so it was just Mark and me. We had the use of their boat, so I was picturing champagne and strawberries and a quiet, romantic boat ride into the middle of this lake, and just as the finale was starting he would lean over and ask me to marry him and I would say yes and there would be an explosion of fireworks while we kissed and the whole world celebrated. Perfect plan for an engagement if you ask me.

Saturday night, about an hour before the fireworks were going to start, Mark and I got some snacks together. We changed, 'cause I was thinking you want to look good when you're getting engaged. Mark got the boat in the water, and then he turned the key. Nothing happened. He tried it again. Nada. The battery was dead.

I thought, *this isn't part of the plan*, and I knew Mark was thinking the same thing 'cause he was scrambling to try to fix the boat. He even tried to take the battery out of my car to use in the boat, but that didn't work so well. Meanwhile, I was trying to come up with an alternative. I had weddings booked for the rest of the summer - I was doing wedding videos on the weekends at that time - so this proposal had to happen tonight, one way or the other.

There was a bridge nearby where all the locals watch the fireworks, so Mark and I headed there. The bridge is only about one hundred yards long and maybe fourteen feet high—just high enough to let power boats go through on the lake. By the time we got there, it was packed, but we found a quiet corner and set up our folding chairs. We had a decent view, and despite the mosquitoes, I was thinking, *this could still work. He can pop the question right before the finale, and we'll still get the fireworks and celebration.* I smiled at Mark. He smiled at me, and we waited for the fireworks to start.

And then a 1970s kidnapper van rolled in. Half of the front windshield was missing, and I knew this because one of the passengers was hanging out the front of the passenger-side windshield.

The van parked illegally on the road, where there was no shoulder, pretty much directly behind Mark and me, about five yards behind us. The side door slid open, and twelve tweens and teens poured out. Even though we had been surrounded by hundreds of people before this, we had built our own little romantic universe. This invasion, however, was impossible to ignore.

First, two of the teenagers sat on the back of the van and played video games, competing over who could make more electronic noise. Then, one of the boys stood right in front of us, just over the tunnel that the boats use, and started fishing. Since boats were still coming through, he had to periodically whip his hook out of the water, leaving me in constant fear for my eyes. Then two of the boys stood behind me and Mark and chucked rocks into the boat-filled lake. Not only was I distracted thinking about all the people in the boats getting pelted, but even worse the kids both had really weak throwing arms—or were actually aiming for us—and so rocks kept landing on Mark and me.

Now Mom—I assumed she was everyone's Mom—Mom was on her cell phone, so she couldn't actually stop talking or leave the van to discipline her children, so she just shouted her commands. "Stop playing those games. Stop throwing rocks." She did not have a problem with the fishing. "Watch the fireworks!"

None of us could ignore her, but her kids did a fantastic job of it. The fireworks, which had started, made it hard for the person on the other end of the call to hear Mom, so she had to talk louder than the fireworks, and this was not a problem for her. Instead of enjoying the light show, Mark and I got sucked into this woman's drama. "If he thinks he's gonna get away with this again, he's got another thing coming. No way that restraining order's gonna stop me this time."

I looked over at Mark, who looked as uncomfortable as I felt, and he just said, "We can leave. Let's just go."

But I don't give up that easily. I put on a smile and said, "No, no, this is great. Let's watch the fireworks." And in my head, I was thinking, *this sucks. But I can't give up now. It has to be tonight. Just wait for the finale.*

As soon as the finale started, Mom started screaming at her rugrats. "Get in the van, now, now. We gotta go, get in the van." Like she was evacuating a war zone. The kids plowed over the rest of us, dropping empty cans and running toward the van. As the last child was literally stepping up into the side door, Mom revved the engine and peeled out, leaving the kid to pull the door shut, once he'd climbed in and as they made a fast U-turn to took off down the road.

No one watched the finale. We were all watching the van depart, and all I could think as they drove off was *there goes my last hope for getting married this year.*

Sunday, Mark and his dad spent the day fixing the boat while I sat on the dock and read. That night, we had a cookout. Any other weekend, it would have been an awesome day. But I was depressed. All I could think about was that our next free weekend was Labor Day, so forget getting married this year.

Monday was a holiday, and I really just wanted to get up and go and not have to sit in traffic until midnight. But Mark loves wakeboarding and hadn't gotten to go yet that summer, so Mark, his dad and mom, and I got on the boat. His dad drove, and

Mark jumped waves for about forty-five minutes while his mom and I watched. Mark finally signaled that he wanted to come in. He handed his board up to his mom and called me over to help him get in the boat.

I was just in a bathing suit, so I awkwardly leaned over the back of the boat, conscious of my derriere up in the air, and put my hand out. Mark took my hand and pulled himself up onto the edge of the boat, and as he stood up, I saw, on the end of his pointer finger, a diamond ring, just resting there, and he said, "Jessica, will you marry me?"

I was looking at the ring on the end of his finger and him on the edge of the boat over a lake and all I could think to say was "How could you take that in the water?!"

He put the ring safely on my finger, and I realized I hadn't given him a proper answer, so I said, "Yes!" Then we started kissing and I was crying with joy and relief. And then I remembered that my ass was in his parents' face and that they were probably wondering why we were making out, so I climbed back into the boat. Mark got in the boat next to me and we shared the news. It was an awesome day.

He'd had the ring tied to his swim trunks while he was wakeboarding, and I found out later that it was a plastic ring anyway, so it wouldn't have mattered much if it fell in the water.

We got married within the year, in September. Three months turned out to be plenty of time to plan a wedding without worrying over the details too much. Mark had, in fact, been going to propose to me on the boat underneath the fireworks that Fourth of July, just as I had suspected. But I'm glad that plans didn't work out that way, because his actual proposal was one of the first, and last, times I can honestly say that I was surprised.

Chapter 20

The Doc

I was sitting in my empty rental—a too big townhouse that belonged to a friend of mine. I'd just left my husband Jake, taking with me everything he let me have—which was pretty much only the stuff I'd owned before meeting him, and my mom's dog, Doc. Doc was providing the soundtrack for my miserable first night alone in seven years.

A thirty-pound border collie mutt with a broken tail that had healed at a horizontal, ninety-degree angle and so much uncontainable energy that he vibrated in place on the rare occasions he wasn't running in circles, Doc paced nervously around the townhouse. His ear-piercing wails of despair echoed—"EeeEeeeeEeee"—making my misery that much more complete. As I stared at him, contemplating murder, I took comfort in the thought that he had to die soon.

Doc had been my mom's dog. She adopted him from a shelter when I was in college. He'd been a year old at the time, had been repeatedly beaten, run over with a car and left for dead. It was a miracle he had lived.

It was his pathetic EeeeEeeee-ing that melted my mom's heart and made her choose him. Of course, once we got him home, we realized he EeeEeeee-ed all the time.

Doc was my mom's constant companion for nine years. Despite whining a lot—though, thankfully, eventually not all the time—he made her very happy. When mom got sick with cancer, she and Doc moved in with me, my husband Jake, and our two eighty-five-pound Labs.

Doc, who was afraid of men generally, and especially men like my husband, who hated him, became an even more tightly wound ball of nerves. My dogs knew how to sit, stay, be quiet, and heel. Doc could not stay still for a second, circling our tiny living room over and over. When we went for our daily walks, he'd try to commit suicide by choking himself the entire time. And then there was his once again ceaseless—EeeeEeeeeeeeing.

My mom died a few months after moving in with us, leaving Doc to me, despite Jake's hatred of the dog. I did my best to reassure Jake he wouldn't have to live with a crazy dog forever. Doc was ten years old. He had to die soon.

A year and a half later, I sat in that mostly empty townhouse, alone for the first time with Doc, hating him for having been the third dog. If we hadn't had him, maybe I could've kept my dogs—my beautiful, perfect, quiet Labs. Instead, I got the problem child, the one that just wouldn't die.

But my mom had loved him, and I figured I might as well make the best of it and try to treat Doc like he was a real dog. I took him running with me, and without the other two dogs to compete with, he could sort of heel, or at least not continuously choke himself. Meal time was less chaotic, since I didn't have to rush Doc to eat his food before the Labs got to it. He always waited until I was eating, so it was like having a dinner companion. Doc slept with me, and he didn't take up the entire bed. We played fetch—kind of. He'd run and get the ball and then drop it about half way back to me—but that was almost a good trick.

And whether it was because Doc became more comfortable around me or he just didn't have my ex-husband or other dogs making him nervous, his whining diminished. He'd still Eeeeeee every time I'd come home, mention going for a walk, start to get his food out, or pick up my keys, but it was no longer incessant, and my ears were able to stop bleeding.

A year later, I bought my own townhouse and got some roommates to help pay the mortgage. They loved Doc. He was crazy, but in an endearing kind of way. Everyone loved when he'd get so excited that his running in circles turned into leaping in circles. And yes, there was whining, but only when he wanted to say he was excited about something—like that Mommy was home. He was so loving, and for the next three years, Doc was my constant companion as roommates and boyfriends came and went.

On my first unofficial, not quite a date with my now husband, Mark, we had a movie night. Doc took to Mark right away, sitting down next to him on the couch. As the movie progressed, Doc decided that some herding was in order. He nudged Mark toward the middle of the couch. Then he climbed over both of us and did the same thing to me so that by the end of the movie, Mark and I were snug up against each other. In that moment, I couldn't have loved Doc more.

When Doc and I moved in with Mark, I got a great man and Doc got a great, big backyard, which he set to patrolling right away. We were one big, happy family.

At sixteen years old, Doc was diagnosed with kidney failure. The vet said he'd probably live only another six months, but by then I didn't believe anything would ever kill him. True to form, it was nearly two years before Doc finally started to slow down. I was six months pregnant when Doc, eighteen years old, stopped eating, getting up, being perpetually in motion.

When Mark and I took him to the vet for what we knew would be the last time, Doc was too weak to stand and had to be carried to the car. Of course, when we got to the vet's office and opened the car door, Doc sprang out and started running in circles, sniffing the grass as if he was as happy as could be. I didn't want to take him inside, but he hadn't eaten or stood up in days, and we knew this was a temporary burst of energy.

In the office, the vet gave us a few minutes alone with Doc. I tried to say comforting things, but mostly just sobbed into his fur. Doc stood and vibrated and whined, and I didn't want him to ever stop.

The vet came in. We tried to get Doc to sit or lay down, but he hadn't learned to do that in eighteen years and wasn't going to now. So, he stood as I held him and they gave him the injection. Thirteen seconds later, he lay down forever.

That first night when it was just me and Doc alone in that big empty townhouse, I was wrong about a lot of things. Most especially, I was wrong in thinking I would be happy when Doc finally died—that he was a burden my mom had left me.

He was my mom's gift to me. He was my dog for eight years, my family, my love until I found my husband, and he was my baby, right up until I had my own little girl. Doc would've loved her—she never sits still either.

Chapter 21

The Recipe

I was nearly thirty when my mom died after a short battle with small-cell lung cancer. My brother, Brian; my sister, Heather; and I were all at her bedside. After she died, we called our dad and told him the news. He said he was sorry, but he didn't offer to make the drive from New Jersey to Virginia to be with us.

My parents got divorced when I was a baby. It wasn't his wife who had died. And we weren't exactly close to our dad. He had a temper. Growing up, I was always afraid of him when he was around. And as each of us got old enough to make those decisions for ourselves, we spent less and less time with our dad. By the time my mom passed away, we didn't have that much of a relationship with him. He chose not to come and be with his kids when their mom had just died, but none of us really expected him to.

Still, a few years later, when my dad was diagnosed with small-cell lung cancer, I started making the drive from Virginia to New Jersey to be with him. I'd go up most weekends and stay for a couple days of the week. I shared duties with Brian and Heather, so I didn't have to be there all the time. When I was there, I tried to be useful. I took Dad to doctor's appointments, to chemo and radiation. I picked up prescriptions and groceries. I tried to do more, like clean and cook. As far as cleaning went, my dad kept his house clean. As far as cooking went, well, my dad was a Piscitelli. Like his brothers and sisters, he was the best cook, so he wouldn't let anyone cook for him because we weren't as good at it as he was.

Dad was sick for four and a half years. I spent a lot of time at his house, and, when I wasn't running him around or running errands, I was always looking for something I could do to best use the time I was there. One day, early on in his illness, when Dad was taking a nap, I decided it was the perfect time to conquer the kitchen cupboard.

My dad's kitchen cupboard looked like he was preparing for World War III. He had canned goods and jars stacked in there that were probably prepared during World War II. I got out a giant trash bag and started digging through. I threw out all the old, expired cans and jars. I guess the noise woke my dad up, because he came into the kitchen. He said, "What the heck are you doing?"

I said, "I'm just getting rid of the bad stuff."

He took a can out of the trash bag and looked at it. He said, "This is fine."

I looked at it and said, "Dad, that expired five years ago."

He said, "Bah! Canned goods don't go bad. They just tell you that so that you'll buy more." Then he started to put the cans back in the cupboard.

I said, "No, Dad. I got this." And I put everything back.

I tried to be useful, but there wasn't a lot to do. And then, about two years in, the cancer started to take its toll. My dad was more tired. He started to have some trouble with words, and started to forget little things. And I realized that there was one thing that I could do better than anyone else in the family. I could capture his stories.

I asked him if he would be okay being interviewed on camera, and he said yes. Before our first interview session, I asked Brian and Heather if they wanted me to ask Dad anything. Heather said no, but Brian said, "Yeah. Ask him for his sauce recipe."

I laughed because Piscitellis don't use recipes.

One weekend, I got the camera set up. I had a list of questions prepared. I got my dad situated on the couch. And when I hit record, I thought, *you know, that's actually a pretty good opening question, a good softball question.* So, I said, "Dad, what's your sauce recipe?"

He laughed and said, "Well, it's not a recipe per se, but uh, you know, you start with the tomatoes. I like to use whole tomatoes. Actually, start with the onions and the garlic. And you know that sauce? That sauce that I make for you guys? That sauce that you guys love so much? I think you love it. Do you love it?"

I said, "Yeah, Dad, we all love your sauce."

He continued, "That is the same sauce that my grandparents made for me when I was growing up. You know, that sauce, they brought that with them when they came from Italy through the Port of New Jersey in 1914. It's the same sauce. I used to spend my summers with them and most weekends. This was back in Paterson, the house they had in Paterson. You know, my grandfather bought that house. It was in the Italian section, so it was cheap. Because the Italians, well, they were legally white by that point, but that doesn't mean anyone wanted to live near them.

"When my grandfather bought that house, it didn't have any plumbing. He had to put it in himself. He put in a back deck up all three stories and ran the plumbing up the deck. It was a four-family house. My grandparents lived on the first floor. My Aunt Mary, she lived in the basement. To get to her door, you had to go down the alley. I was this scrawny little kid, and I had to squeeze between these two buildings to fit down that alley."

My dad was no longer in the room. He was in his childhood.

"I spent my summers there, and every weekend. On Saturdays, every Saturday, other than in the winter, we spent the day canning and preserving and just saving anything we could, you know, anything my grandmother could grow in her little postage stamp garden. It was this little four by four. It's amazing how much stuff she could grow. Then my grandfather, he'd go out to the farmer's market—it wasn't called that back then—but he'd go out and he'd get a bushel of peaches or whatever was cheap, you know, about to go bad, and we'd preserve that too. I didn't know it at the time, but it was survival.

"And then on Sunday, after Mass, we'd go back to the house, and the whole house, the whole neighborhood, the smell of garlic would just hit you in the face. That's where Italians got the reputation for being stinky. Americans didn't cook with garlic and onion. But everyone in the neighborhood was doing the same thing my grandparents were doing. They were getting out they're big pots, and then my grandmother, she'd throw in the garlic and onion and tomatoes and whatever she had on hand. She'd put in whatever she could get from the garden, whatever we had preserved. Sometimes my grandfather, he'd go and he'd get some chickens—I'm talking live chickens, right? And he'd butcher one for the sauce, and then he'd butcher the rest and freeze it.

"We were dirt-poor, but man did we eat good. Those are the best memories I have of my childhood."

My dad's throat caught a little at the end. He had to take a lot of breaks. He'd go get another cup of coffee or let the dog out. Really, I think he just didn't want me to see him get emotional.

We didn't finish the interview in one weekend. I brought my camera with me whenever I'd visit and set it up when we had time or when my dad had the energy.

Over time, my dad let me in the kitchen again. I'd cook, under his supervision. He'd say, "Put a little more oregano in." So, I'd put a little more oregano in, and he'd say, "Bah! What the heck are you doing?! I said a *little* bit more."

I said, "Dad, I did."

He said, "It's fine. It'll be fine." And it was.

The next time I sat my dad down in front of the camera, I realized I hadn't actually gotten the sauce recipe. So, I started there again. I said, "Dad, what's your sauce recipe?"

He laughed again and said, "Uh, you know, when I married your mother, she couldn't boil an egg. I had to teach her everything about how to cook. I don't know that she ever learned. But those years that we were living in Clifton, it was just me and your mother and Brian." He paused, then explained, "Your brother."

I said, "Yeah, Dad, I know who Brian is."

He continued, "Yeah, well, those were some good years. I did a lot of cooking those first few years. I remember this one day, I called up my cousin and I said 'Hey, what's grandma and grandpa's sauce recipe?' And he said, 'What? Are you trying to get back to being Italian?' And I said, 'Yeah. Maybe I am.' Because, you know, your grandma, my mother, she was an immigrant too, but from Canada. In other words, she was white. So, they raised us kids to be white. When I think back on all those years, I think about all that heritage I missed out on."

Dad spent a minute lost in thought before continuing. "But those first couple years with your mother, those were good times. And then I don't know what happened. You know, Heather came along, and I was working twelve-, thirteen-hour days. I'd get home, and I just wanted to eat and go to bed. But Brian was toddling around knocking stuff over, and the baby was crying, and the house was always a mess. I mean, your mother didn't even have a job. What was she doing all day? And I just felt like I had to be the father, you know? I turned into a dictator."

My dad paused, taking a sip of coffee. "You know, I was afraid of my father until I was in my thirties. I was hanging out with a buddy, having a drink, and I guess I said something about my father, and my buddy, he said, 'Don't tell me that you're still afraid of that little Guinea.' And I thought about it, and I realized I was six, seven inches taller than my dad. I could step on him and squash him like a grape if I wanted to. And that's when I stopped being afraid of him. But growing up, you know, I was the oldest, the firstborn. I wouldn't say that I raised my brothers and sisters, but I was responsible for them. Well, for the original six, as I like to call them. The other three came along later. But, you know, my dad, he'd get home after working a fifteen-to-sixteen-hour days at the factory, and he just wanted it to be quiet. He wanted to eat in peace and quiet. And God help you if you disturbed him. But if you could stare him down, if you could deny it, you could avoid getting smacked. And my brothers and sisters, they were great at staring him down, but they were my responsibility, capesce?

"I remember one day, this is when your grandpa was older, not long before he died, and we were sitting around the table and he looked at me and said, 'Was I really that bad?' I said, 'Yeah, Dad, you were.' And he didn't say anything. He just got up and walked away and didn't come back out of his room that night. You know, he never asked me for forgiveness, but I knew that he regretted some things and I forgave him."

"Those years, those first few years with your mother and your brother, those were the happiest years of my life. And then, I don't know what happened. I just turned into my father. I probably should have come and been with you kids when your mother died."

My dad had to go get himself another cup of coffee, and we picked up recording on another weekend.

You know, my dad never asked me for forgiveness, at least not directly, but I forgave him. I never did get that sauce recipe though. But, you know, eventually my dad actually allowed me to do the cooking. He even complimented me a few times, so I guess I learned what I needed to know. I never got the recipe, but Piscitellis don't use recipes anyway.

Chapter 22

A Lesson in Biology

I was a good student in high school. I listened in class, even in sex ed. I learned early on how babies are made. It's really very simple. The man puts his penis in the woman's vagina, and nine months later a baby pops out of that same vagina. Easy-peasy.

In the decades since I took that class, a few things have changed. There've been a lot of medical advances in how we deal with pregnancy, changes to what tests are standard during pregnancy, and there's been a global change in fertility rates; specifically, infertility rates are going up.

On a more personal level, thankfully, when I was in high school, I had no desire for a baby. That changed, almost exactly on the day I turned thirty. It was like everyone yelled happy birthday and then suddenly I started hearing this ticking and feeling this twinge, and every part of my body started screaming, *it's baby making time!*

And that's when I realized I was not in a good place to make a baby. I was married to a man who didn't treat me well. More than anything, I knew I did not want to make a baby with him.

Turns out divorcing, recovering from divorcing, and finding a man whom you *do* want to have a baby with, and who wants to make a baby with you, takes a little bit of time. When my new and improved husband, Mark, and I got engaged, I was thirty-six years old. Since we wanted two kids, we started trying to get pregnant right away, you know, the good old-fashioned way. And that was fun, 'cause we tried a lot. We really gave it our all.

Eight months later, I had my annual OB-GYN exam. I love Dr. Clark, if it's possible to love someone who uses a speculum on you every time you see them. She is quirky and weird and a little inappropriate.

When my exam was over, Dr. Clark said, "Everything looks good. We'll send you a postcard with results, because who doesn't love getting a postcard?" Then she asked, "Is there anything you want to discuss?"

Now, I'd done a bit of googling, making me a minor expert on all things baby making, so I knew couples were considered infertile when they'd been trying unsuccessfully for over a year. Still, since I was there and all, I said, "My husband and I have been trying to get pregnant—it's only been about eight months, and I know you're supposed to wait a year before . . . "

She cut me off saying, "Oh no, when you're as old as you are, we test for infertility after six months." Thanks for putting that so delicately!

After the first round of tests, it turned out that there was very little chance Mark and I would be able to make a baby without medical assistance. Despite our having no religious or other biases about getting help from the medical community, there was just something that felt unnatural in the idea of making a baby in a lab. Maybe it was simply the fact that men and women had been making babies by making love for thousands of years. I wanted it to be that easy and, frankly, fun for us. But if Mark and I wanted to have children made from us, modern medicine was going to have to take over the process. And we did, at least, want to give this newfangled baby making a try before considering other options.

We went to an infertility clinic in Maryland. Did they have to call it that? As if you weren't aware that your problem was infertility—you get to be reminded of it every step of the way. Every practice, hospital, doctor, what have you, refers to it as infertility treatments, so it wasn't just this clinic. Still, from the moment Mark and I walked into that office building, every step felt clinical.

After we were issued our official baby-making photo IDs, the clinic ran more fertility tests to make sure we'd be able to produce babies, if they decided to help us. Then they tested our finances, to make sure we'd be able to pay for the process. Finally, they tested our genes, to make sure we could make perfect babies.

Once all the formalities were out of the way, Mark and I were scheduled to meet with the doctor that they assigned to us, Dr. Blue.

Dr. Blue started off the meeting by explaining how babies are made, the new way. She went over the à la carte options, making sure we understood what each one involved. For a granola lover like me, none of the choices seemed good. We were talking about making a baby using my body, and I wanted it to be as organic a process as possible.

I tried to keep it light while explaining where I was coming from, "I'd like to try to do this in as natural a manner as possible, with the least amount of drugs. I just don't like too many chemicals. I mean, I eat organic, more to the point, non-GMO food, ya know?"

Dr. Blue did not find me amusing, but she did suggest that we start trying for a baby with IUI, intrauterine insemination, which is as close to how babies are made in nature as we were gonna get. In IUI, they place the sperm into the uterus via, essentially, a turkey baster. It's kinda like having sex—just without the fun.

Mark and I agreed to move forward, and over the next four

months we tried IUI three times and failed to get pregnant all three times. The staff at the clinic scheduled another meeting with Dr. Blue to discuss the next step in the baby-making process, IVF, in vitro fertilization.

We hadn't seen Dr. Blue since that first consultation, so I was surprised when she called me a few days before our scheduled appointment. I was even more surprised by what she said.

"Sorry to tell you this, but since you are a carrier for the fragile X gene, you can't begin the IVF process until you speak with a genetic counselor."

This was the first I was hearing of this. I said, "I don't understand. We got tested for everything…"

She cut me off saying, "You'll have to speak with the genetic counselor about it. I'm sorry. Call the office to make an appointment."

And then she hung up, as if not wanting to wait for understanding to sink in, the understanding that we weren't going to be allowed to proceed.

I couldn't speak to the counselor until the next day, so it was a long night of worrying about what this could mean for our baby-making plans. But as with so much with this process, there was nothing I could do but wait and worry.

The counselor called the next day and said, "I don't understand why you called."

"Our doctor said we were carriers for fragile X."

"Yes, I know, I got your message, but I don't know why. Did you get another test done?"

"Not that I know of."

"Our records show you and your husband are not carriers. You wouldn't have been able to do the IUIs if you were. I think you need to talk to your doctor again, because I don't know where she's getting this information from. It's not from us."

I was somewhat relieved, but also confused, because Lord knows we had taken enough tests. Maybe, at some point, something had turned up that the counselor wasn't aware of.

I called the clinic right away to try to sort it out. The nurse—you can never get the doctor—the nurse who called me back said, "I think Dr. Blue must have called you by mistake. She probably had the wrong file in front of her."

"Are you sure? I want to be sure that there's nothing wrong. Can you please have Dr. Blue call us again?"

The nurse said "I have an email out to Dr. Blue. I'm sure it was just a simple mistake, but I'll let Dr. Blue know to call."

After a week of not hearing back we went to a new clinic, Virginia Fertility.

I loved Dr. Petersen right away, if you can love someone who is like your ob-gyn on crack, as far as your vagina is concerned. He was tall and soft-spoken and took time to listen to our concerns. He suggested IVF, and, as we were already prepared for that suggestion, we agreed.

I gotta tell you, there is nothing natural about IVF. In IVF, the doctors harvest the woman's eggs and the man's sperm, whisk them together in a dish, and stick the resulting embryo in utero! In order for them to get lots of eggs for the baby batter, I had to put so many hormones in me that I will never be allowed to work at Whole Foods.

For about three weeks I injected stimulating hormones, twice a day, in my belly. The needles burned, but the stimulating hormones drove me crazy—like my worst teenage period ever, times one thousand crazy. I would literally cry at the drop of a hat or spilt milk. I was physically sensitive, bloated, crampy, gaining weight, feeling hot and anxious and generally miserable.

In addition to injecting needles into my belly, I regularly got my blood drawn, so my arms and belly were covered in small bruises. And then, of course, there was the persistent wanding, and unfortunately, I am not talking about the magical, wizarding-world kind of wand—though this one could see really well inside my uterus, which is kind of like magic.

But Mark and I were hopeful this method would succeed, so we were willing to go through the torture, and by "we" I do mostly mean "me." I mean, Mark had to put up with me being all hormonal and cranky, but he got off pretty easy compared with the discomfort I had to put up with. If you think about it, that, at least, is how baby making normally goes.

Finally, the bloodwork and the wanding revealed that the time was ripe, and so was I. The big day was here: egg-retrieval day.

The morning of the procedure I was nervous when we got to the doctor's office, but the nurse gave me a mild sedative. As the nurse walked me over to the gurney, she said, "Someone's getting happy." It wasn't that clever, but I thought it was the funniest thing ever. Yeah, it was a good drug.

She wheeled me into the operating room—which was just another room in the doctor's office—and strapped my legs into the stirrups at an almost ninety-degree angle. She was just saying the doctor would be in in a minute when the fire alarm went off.

The nurse said, "I'll be right back," and she left, leaving the door open. I was naked but for a hospital gown, strapped to a gurney with my legs spread very wide, and now the room was filling with smoke. It occurred to me that I might die in a rather embarrassing way.

I kept picturing the firemen coming in and finding me like that, which, of course, I found hysterical.

Moments later, the nurse and Dr. Petersen came in, closing the door, and the nurse quickly explained that an AC unit had caught fire and it was nothing to worry about. Un-sedated, I might have thought that an electrical fire is something to worry about. Instead, I just smiled and said, "Okay." I was feeling no pain—until of course, the procedure began. The happy pill did not help with the pain of having my eggs cut out or with what they described as the mild cramping that followed.

I survived—the procedure and the electrical fire—and the good news is they were able to produce nine viable embryos.

I had to return to the office five days later with a full bladder. I am a good student. I showed up to the office with a full bladder. It felt like someone had stuck a garden hose in my belly button and turned it on. I was afraid it was going to start coming out my eyes.

When the nurse came to get me, she asked, "Is your bladder full?"

"Oh yeah, I'm going to explode any second."

"Oh," she said, "That might be a little too full. Go into the bathroom and pee, just a little. About a cup's worth."

I imagined myself a dam. I was supposed to crack the dam open and let out just a little water before closing it back up. I was afraid I wouldn't be able to stop if I let it go, so I ended up not relieving much of the pressure.

I was still pretty close to bursting. When I lay down, they put cold gel on my belly, then pressed and held down my bladder while the doctor inserted two embryos. The whole procedure took maybe two minutes, which was good, 'cause I really needed to relieve myself, but then the nurse said, "Just lie still for ten more minutes, and then you can go pee."

That was the longest wait in my life. Longer than the two weeks we had to wait to find out if it worked.

Two weeks later, I went in for bloodwork in the morning. The nurse called me that afternoon. When I picked up the phone she asked, "How are you?"

"I don't know. How am I?"

She said, "You are excited and happy."

She was right. One embryo took, and I was so excited to find out I was pregnant. Mark and I—and the nurses, and the doctors, and the lab assistants—had done it. We had made a baby!

Then the nurse said, "And remember, no sex or orgasms for twelve weeks."

"What? Did you say no sex for twelve days?"

"No sex OR orgasms for twelve weeks."

That was the longest wait of my life!

A lot has changed since I took that sex ed. class all those years ago. For that, I am eternally grateful.

Chapter 23

What Are the Odds

Having a baby is easy. Right? I mean, everyone does it. Eighty-one percent of women become mothers at some point. That's a lot of people having babies.

By contrast, I have run marathons. Only 0.5 percent of the population has done that—because it's hard. Hence, the way I saw it, having a baby must be easy.

Of course, when I did get pregnant, I found out very quickly that pregnancy is not easy. I think all 81 percent of the women who've had babies will agree with me on that one. Unlike most of those women, however, I had a uniquely challenging pregnancy, with the stats to prove it.

Since 80 percent of miscarriages happen in the first twelve weeks, we decided not to go public until we reached that benchmark, which was hard for me—because I got very pregnant very fast. I was nauseous and dizzy and faint and felt exhausted. I wanted to be able to share with my friends that there was actually a really good reason for my rapid weight gain.

The twelve weeks passed, which was great for a couple reasons.

I got an ultrasound in my ob-gyn office, and everything looked good. It was so amazing, seeing the little life growing inside me. In fact, the doctor and Mark and I all thought we saw a penis on the monitor. I asked the doctor if he thought we were having a boy.

He said "There's a good chance of it."

"Really?"

"Yep. I would say at least 50 percent!"

Ah, doctor humor.

Boy or girl, I was relieved to finally be able to share the good news with my family and friends. To me, it was like we had passed go. We were having a baby, and nothing could take that away now.

At twenty weeks, they give you what's called a level-two ultrasound to make sure the baby is the expected size and shape and that all of their organs are in the right place. Once you pass that test, it's usually smooth sailing.

Because it's the big benchmark, a lot of people get nervous about this test, but I already felt like I had a healthy little boy growing inside me. He was so active, kicking and punching me all day and night. There couldn't possibly be a concern.

Mark took off of work early and picked me up, and we went to our three o'clock appointment at Fairfax Radiology. Remember how active the baby was? That made the ultrasound last over an hour. The technician was chasing that thing around my belly trying to get all the measurements. She was actually getting frustrated. "Your baby moves too much."

I smiled at Mark. He'd heard me complain about that about a million times already.

A little while later she said, "Do you know the sex?"

"We think it's a boy."

"Do you want me to tell you?"

"Yeah."

"You are having a girl."

There was magic in that moment. Not that we would have cared more one way or the other, but knowing that the creature in my belly was a little girl made it so real. It was a she, a little girl, not just an embryo.

The technician left us to get the radiologist. Mark and I held hands, tears in our eyes as we imagined the baby girl we'd be raising.

The radiologist came in and started taking more images. She didn't seem frustrated. She seemed concerned.

"Is anything wrong?" I asked.

"Let me finish this and then we'll talk." That wasn't the no I was looking for.

By the time she was done and I had changed back into my clothes, it was after 5:00 p.m., and the place was a ghost town.

The radiologist said, "There's more calcification in your baby's heart than we like to see."

"What does that mean?"

"You will need to talk to your doctor about it. I tried calling, but the office is closed. I will call them first thing tomorrow and suggest you do the same."

"Is our baby okay?" I asked, trying to keep the note of rising panic out of my voice.

"Your doctor will discuss it with you."

Not a yes.

After giving us what seemed like scary news but no concrete information, she said just about the dumbest thing a person has ever said to me.

"Go home and relax." As if that weren't enough, she added, "And whatever you do, don't google it!"

Had she never heard of reverse psychology? As soon as we got in the car, I googled it. In her defense, I wish I had listened to her.

What I found was Down syndrome, heart defects, and fetal death. Stillborn babies with calcification in their hearts.

What should've been a happy day—finding out we were having a girl, telling everyone about it—turned out to be a horrible night, filled with me refusing to answer my phone and imagining my baby dying.

Mark said, "We don't know anything and shouldn't jump to conclusions." But all I could think about were the baby autopsy reports I'd seen linked to the articles I'd perused.

The next morning, I waited impatiently for it to be 9:05 a.m., and then I called my doctor's office. I left a message. An hour later, when they still hadn't called, I phoned Fairfax Radiology.

"Yes, the radiologist said she was going to call my doctor this morning? Oh, she did? At 8:30 a.m. Thanks."

I called my ob-gyn office again. I had to leave another message. "I'm trying to talk with a doctor about my ultrasound. I would just like to find out what next steps are and it sounds like something's wrong and I need to know what's going on and you need to call me back." This time, there was full-on panic in my voice.

A million years later, at 12:30 p.m., a doctor from the ob-gyn office called and apologized, saying they were short-staffed.

She said, "The calcification in your baby's heart are called echogenic foci. Most babies have a little calcification, but yours has a few more spots than we like to see. It could indicate a heart defect or a genetic disorder. I've scheduled you to get a fetal EKG at a pediatric cardiologist as well as another ultrasound at Fairfax Hospital's antenatal unit."

My head was spinning, but Google had nothing new to offer.

A few nail-biting days later, Mark and I went to the heart specialist's office for a fetal EKG. This tech also had trouble chasing my baby around my belly. It took a long time, hours, and she wasn't convinced she ever got a clean image. After she was done, or gave up, not sure which, Mark and I sat down with the pediatric cardiologist, Dr. S. An intense, middle-aged woman, she had the manner of someone pretending to be cheerful, which made me even more uncomfortable than I already was.

She drew us a sketch of the heart as she explained the results. "The foci are located along the pulmonary wall, leading me to believe that what we are seeing are just thicker areas of the heart muscle."

"Does that mean our baby's okay?"

"I can't be 100 percent sure, but if I were a betting woman, I would bet on this being nothing to worry about."

I can't tell you how relieved I was. I had been trying not to live in fear over the past few days—because stress is bad for the baby—but mostly I'd been failing. Now I could breathe again, tell everyone we were having a girl. Just to be safe, the doctor's office scheduled us for a follow-up in a month.

In the meantime, Mark and I went to the ultrasound appointment we already had scheduled at the hospital. I wasn't worried about this appointment anymore. I mean, the heart specialist was betting on my baby girl being fine, so I was looking at this as another chance to see her moving around.

As the tech started my ultrasound, she asked why we were there. I explained about the foci and how the cardiologist had said it was nothing to worry about. After about ten minutes, the tech stepped out into the hall and called a nurse into the room. Even though they were talking to each other in the corner, I could hear them perfectly.

The tech showed the nurse the monitor and said, "They told them there was nothing to worry about." The nurse said, "I'll call the cardiologist right away."

I said, "What's going on?"

"The doctor will explain when she gets here."

I was getting sick of being told that.

The nurse and technician had nothing good to say about the fact that Dr. S had missed something, but since they wouldn't tell me what was going on with my baby, I didn't care about their opinion of the heart specialist.

The cardiologist on-site was from the same office as Dr. S. After more imaging with her portable EKG machine, I sat up, and this cardiologist told me the new news. Completely unrelated to the foci, my baby girl had a hole in her heart, called a VSD. It's a small opening between the two chambers of the heart. Sometimes a VSD will close on its own. Sometimes, it never closes but turns out not to be a problem. Sometimes, it requires heart surgery. It was too soon to know. We would have to monitor its progress.

The nurse and doctor and technician all had a power-play moment and wanted to fight about who was the smartest person in the room as they discussed taking more images of my belly, but we'd been at the hospital for four and a half hours, and when I went to lay back down, I fainted.

If you ever want to get out of a test, I highly recommend being pregnant and fainting. Not only did I get out of the test, but they gave me graham crackers and apple juice and sent me home.

This doctor had made it seem like the VSD wasn't a big concern. I was determined not to worry. When you have a baby in your belly, everything transfers, even stress. And stress can cause all sorts of problems for a baby. I tried to think happy thoughts and focus them on my little girl.

It was in this short period, between doctor visits, while thinking happy thoughts, that a name came to me. It was so perfect; I knew it had to be hers. When I told Mark, he got tears in his eyes. At twenty-two weeks, we named our baby girl. We decided not to share her name with anyone until she was born.

At twenty-four weeks, we went back for the follow-up with Dr. S. After another EKG, we had another consultation. This time, there was no fake smile.

Dr S. began, "The tumors in her heart..."

I interrupted, "Wait, they're tumors now?!"

She took a deep breath and continued, "There are two kinds of tumors they could be. Neither is cancerous. A fibroma continues to grow as the fetus grows. They need to be removed before they interfere with heart function."

My mind was reeling, my heart pounding. "You mean like open-heart surgery? Like after she's born?"

"Let's not even go down that path unless we have to." Dr. S. took another deep breath, a pause, before continuing. "The other kind of tumor, rhabdomyoma, will stop growing and eventually shrink until they are not a problem. However, rhabdomyomas are an indication of a genetic disorder called tuberous sclerosis, or TS. At this time, we can't tell which type of tumors she has."

Mark and I left the office in silence. I felt shell-shocked.

After more misguided googling, the way I saw it, we had two bad possibilities. The one kind of tumor could grow until it stopped her heart. The other kind could mean she'd have a genetic disorder with symptoms like autism, seizures, and continuous tuberous growths in her heart, kidneys, and brain.

The amazing thing is that both types of tumor are extremely rare. Only one in ten thousand babies gets either. That's 0.01 percent. If I were Dr. S, I would've bet against those odds too.

All we could do was wait and go to more appointments. The next day, we had to meet with a genetic specialist. I tell you; we were getting around.

The geneticist was a young woman with a sweet nature, who was very pregnant. She asked us a long list of questions about family health history, none of which helped explain the tumors or the hole in my baby's heart.

She couldn't really answer any questions for us. If it was TS, tests could not be run until after she was born, so the appointment felt like a waste of time. But before we left, there was one more bomb to drop.

"If you choose, you could still terminate the pregnancy."

"Are you saying we should? I mean, are you advising us to?"

"No. I am just letting you know; it is still an option. Not in Virginia, but in other states."

"Are you saying that it's the best option?"

"I am not saying that—just letting you know because you have to decide soon."

In that moment I realized that the odds were really against us, that my baby girl might not make it. And the thought of her dying inside me horrified me.

Even though I hadn't met her face-to-face yet, I loved her. She was my little girl, and she was real to me. She was with me at all times, and I had no choice but to think about her constantly.

I loved her, but I was terrified of what it would do to me— falling even more in love with her over the next several months, only to have her die before she was born or, worse, in my arms.

The way I saw it, she had a 50 percent chance of dying—of the tumors being the fibromas that would grow until they stopped her heart. Because, of course, that's what I imagined happening.

If she got the other type of tumor, her odds got crazy: 0.01 percent of the population get tumors on their hearts. Of those, half have rhabdomyomas. Of those, 80 percent get tuberous sclerosis. Of those, some live very normal lives, and a small percent die from a tumor growing in their brain or heart.

In the seconds that passed after the geneticist said the words "terminate the pregnancy," all the worst images played out in my mind. I could not bear the idea of carrying this life one day more if I was going to have to watch her die. Nor could I bear the idea of making the choice to end her life.

Mark and I took a moment. That was all we needed. As much as it seemed like the odds were against us, we decided to bet on our baby girl to survive.

At thirty weeks, we went in for another appointment with Dr. S. She said, somewhat cheerfully, "The tumors haven't gotten any bigger."

Even though that sounded positive, I felt like Dr. S didn't

understand what Mark and I were going through, didn't understand how much we were hanging on her words, so I said, "We haven't been preparing for having a baby—we didn't set up the baby's room or throw a shower—because we haven't known if we are having this baby. Do these results mean we can go ahead and start preparing?"

Dr. S thought for a long time before answering. "It would be better if you wait until after our next appointment."

So, no—the answer was no. We shouldn't let ourselves believe we were having a baby.

Our baby was due in ten weeks, and we still were unable to plan for her.

Not that it wasn't hard for Mark, because it was, but for me, there was no escape. Every time she kicked me—which was often—I worried, incorrectly, that her being so active might be a sign of TS. And as we both grew bigger, my fear grew, but I had no way of hiding.

When you are obviously pregnant, everyone is happy for you. Complete strangers would smile at me and ask "When are you due?" Or "How far along are you?" Or, the one that hurt the most, "Boy or girl?"

I'd force myself to smile back and say, "I'm having a girl," and try to believe it.

Somehow, the next month passed. I had bad days, when I cried, thought terrible thoughts, and filled my body and my baby with stress. I had good days, when I managed not to think at all. And then it was June. And another meeting with the cardiologist.

The results of the EKG, six weeks before my baby was due, showed that she still had tumors on her heart, but they had not grown, and might have shrunk.

"Does that mean they are rhabdomyomas?"

"We still can't be sure, but it is more likely."

And with minimal fanfare, Dr. S announced, "You are having

a baby."

I did feel a sense of relief, but I still couldn't breathe, not until I was sure my baby was safe and healthy.

There was one positive outcome from this appointment. My friends were throwing us a baby shower that weekend. I'd told them they could go ahead and plan it, and if we got bad news, people would understand if we canceled. I was excited that we were finally going to get to celebrate this little girl growing inside me.

The next day, however, I had another appointment at Fairfax Hospital. Thanks to being placed on the dangerous-pregnancy watchlist, I was a regular there. This time, unlike most of my visits, the doctor called me into her office after my tests.

"We like to see amniotic fluid levels of around nine. Yours have dropped closer to six. I'm putting you on bed rest for the weekend and then want you back here on Monday for more testing."

Now, of course, I took this very seriously. But *this* weekend? Really? "We're having our baby shower this weekend. I'd really like to go. I kinda need to go."

She gave me a hard, stern stare. I could tell she was judging me. My kid wasn't even born yet and someone already thought I was a bad parent.

"Fine. But no driving, stay seated, have people bring you drinks and food and presents, and whatever you do, don't stress yourself."

Ha! Now she tells me.

I was having a baby in six weeks and was planning to take off three months from work after the baby was born. For my remaining pregnancy, I was put on bed rest with orders not to work, except for my new, unpaid, full-time job of going to doctors at least three times a week.

I could tell that my baby girl was unhappy with all the tests too. She took a particular dislike to the fetal heart rate monitor. They strapped a belt around my belly with, essentially, a microphone pointed at my baby's heart. They turned on the monitor nice and loud and let the beat drop. After a couple minutes, my little girl honed in on whatever it was that was poking into her space and started to use it as a punching bag. THAT noise amplified really well, scaring the other mamas. She was persistent too, so that eventually, every time I walked in, the nurse turned the audio down as soon as she had me hooked up.

And, of course, because nothing about this pregnancy could be easy or normal, it was around this time that my baby girl sat down, head up, legs in a vee, feet by her face, in breech—and refused to move. Not that I was looking forward to pushing a baby out of my vagina, but I'd thought that in that one way at least, I could go low-tech and natural. A breech baby, in this day and age, means a C-section.

We had one final prenatal EKG, a week before the scheduled C-section. When we got to our appointment, Dr. S was no longer with the practice.

The new cardiologist who met with us was just the right balance of serious and laid-back you look for in a doctor.

He said, "The fact that the tumors are shrinking leads us to conclude that they are rhabdomyomas. My guess is they will continue to shrink and eventually become so small that they're a nonissue. The VSD has all but disappeared. We do need to check her again after she's born because the heart changes after birth, but as far as cardiology is concerned, it looks good."

"Um. Okay. What about the tuberous sclerosis?"

"You'll have to see a specialist for that after she's born. I can tell you that the majority of babies we see with these types of tumors test negative for TS."

I don't know if it was the news he gave us or the way he gave us the news, but when we left, I finally felt like I could breathe.

Early one July morning, as soon as Dr. Clark made the final incision, my baby girl launched herself, feetfirst out of my womb and into the world.

A few minutes, and a few tests, later, Mark placed the little girl we'd named Hope on my heart. If I'd been in love with her before she was born, I was so much more in love from the moment I met her face-to-face. I held Hope in my arms and knew, no matter what any tests said, that my little girl was perfect.

A week after Hope was born, we went back to the cardiologist. The hole in her heart had disappeared. The tumors had shrunk. The cardiologist pronounced her heart *normal.*

TS is a hard disease to rule out. Hope's had a million tests, and they've all come back negative, but only time will really tell.

I haven't bothered to google or crunch the numbers. The way I see it, the only thing I can be 100 percent sure of is that I am blessed to have Hope.

Chapter 24

Butterball

We got pregnant with our baby girl on our first round of IVF. Our fertility doctor, Dr. Petersen, implanted two embryos, and one of them took. We had seven frozen embryos left.

Mark and I wanted two kids. They could play with each other. Take care of each other. Grow up together. Shortly after our baby girl Hope's first birthday, we started trying for baby number two.

I guess since the IVF had worked the first time with Hope, we got a little cocky and decided to put only one embryo in this time. Or, as Dr. Petersen put it, we decided to "minimize the risk of twins." We really wanted only one more kid; two would be a lot.

The process this time was a little streamlined because they already had embryos. But there were some needles and some hormones and a full bladder and then that two-week wait. After all the stress we went through with everything going wrong with my first pregnancy, I was still somehow surprised and disappointed when this initial attempt to get pregnant failed.

For our second round, we went full tilt and put in two embryos, trying to stack the deck a little. When our second attempt failed, I started to get nervous. We were down to four embryos, and I wasn't getting any younger.

I met with Dr. Petersen, who said, "We could try a new procedure. I would do a biopsy of your uterus. We would check to make sure there are no lingering infections, but moreover, we've found that statistically, successful pregnancy rates go up in the month after we've performed the biopsy."

I was already fully committed to this process, so I agreed to try it. The biopsy hurt. Unlike during the egg retrieval, there were no sedatives, and Dr. Petersen basically gave me a paper cut on the inside of my womb. But it was worth it—or it would have been—if the next two embryos had taken.

We had only two embryos left and no other tricks to try. More needles, more hormones, more timing. We put both embryos in and waited to find out if this last chance would work.

It's not that we couldn't try to make more embryos, but we had a one-and-a-half-year-old, I was almost forty, and I'd been doing hormone injections for nearly six months and was physically and mentally exhausted. Did I mention the one-and-a-half-year-old? Mark and I held our breath for the next two weeks. Well, almost two weeks.

The day before I was due for my bloodwork was a Sunday. When I was getting breakfast ready, I dropped and broke a bowl. A little while later I spilled a glass of water. And then, when we were outside playing with Hope, I just fell over. For no reason. When Mark came to help me up, I said, "I think I'm pregnant."

He said, "It certainly seems that way."

The next day, we confirmed baby number two was in the cooker.

You'd think that's the happy ending to this story. What's crazy is that I thought that was the happy ending, even though I should've known by now that baby making is never that simple.

With fertility treatments, the doctors don't congratulate you right away. They keep testing you.

Two days later, my bloodwork showed my beta levels had doubled—a good sign. But four days after that, my beta levels were lower than normal.

I had to go back in two days for more bloodwork and my old friend the wand. Dr. Petersen was out that day, so the female doctor who was there operated the wand. I gotta say, women doctors are less gentle with the wand than the men. It's almost like she was thinking *I gotta deal with this myself. You can just suck it up.* And men were always a little more like *Oh, I'm so sorry I have to do this. I'll go easy.*

Anyway, after some not-so-gentle wanding, this lady doctor said, "The embryo is smaller than we'd like it to be."

I started deflating right away. I could guess where this was going, so I didn't ask any questions. She added, "Come back in a week, when Dr. Petersen is here. He knows your body better, so maybe he'll see something that I'm not."

Over the next week, against all better judgment, which I lacked completely, I googled it and got a resounding diagnosis of "imminent miscarriage." I was depressed but determined to not think about it too much, which, I gotta say, is a lot easier to do when you have a one-and-a-half-year-old to distract you.

At my return visit, after more bloodwork and wanding, Dr. Petersen said, "The beta levels have risen sluggishly. The sac"—what he was now calling the embryo—"the sac has not shown enough growth. I can't consider this a normal pregnancy. I'm sorry, but you should expect to miscarry in one to two weeks."

I wasn't surprised, but hearing the words still hurt.

"This is definitely not happening? I can go off the hormones and drink alcohol and have sex?" Because, you know, there's gotta be some compensation for this kinda news.

"I really can't see a way that this pregnancy is going to happen, so feel free to do all of that. I'll want to check you again in a week, if you haven't miscarried."

I was crushed, of course. We wanted this baby. And I really didn't want to go through the process of trying to make new embryos or trying to begin to figure out the adoption process. We didn't have a plan for if this didn't work, and I didn't want to have to come up with one.

On the upside, it was a relief to *know*. I didn't have to imagine the worst happening. Dr. Petersen already pretty much told me to expect the worst. Still, it wasn't over yet. There was more waiting. Waiting for a miscarriage.

It was weird, waiting for the life I'd hoped for so much to end. I didn't want it to end, but I knew it was going to, and since it was going to, I wanted to get it over with so I could grieve and move on. And from a practical point of view, I was going to Montana for work in a week and a half and really didn't want to have a miscarriage while on a plane or while away from home.

But I didn't have the miscarriage that week and had to go back in to see Dr. Petersen two days before my business trip. Mark offered to come to the appointment with me. I said, "Why bother? It's not like we're gonna find out anything new."

Ha. Apparently, I still hadn't learned that there is always the possibility of a curveball.

While I lie there, with the wand inside me, Dr. Petersen stared at the monitor for a long, uncomfortable time, his face unreadable. Finally, I called, "Hey, uh, what's going on down there?"

He turned the monitor to face me, and pointed to the screen. "See that? It's an embryo. And it has a heartbeat."

Uh, what?

"I don't want to get your hopes up, which is why I wasn't saying anything. You might still miscarry. But there is a chance—a slim chance—that this will turn out to be a normal pregnancy after all. I'd like to check you again in another week, if you haven't miscarried."

Boom. A week ago, I'd been miserable at the news I would lose the baby. Now I was—I didn't know what I was. Miserable, because we were back to not knowing what was going to happen. I don't like not knowing. Scared. Verging on hopeful. It was one very confusing week.

I went to Montana and did not miscarry on the plane or while away. I got back late Friday night.

Even though the clinic doesn't normally take monitoring patients on Saturdays, Dr. Petersen was sympathetic and agreed to see me Saturday morning so I wouldn't have to wait until Monday to find out what was going on. This time, Mark came along.

As I was lying on the table, Mark holding my hand, wand in its usual place of honor, Dr. Petersen turned the audio on the monitor up and asked, "You know what that is?"

I'd had enough drama over the last couple weeks, and I didn't need any more dramatic tension, so I was maybe a little snippy with my response. "It's a heartbeat! What does that mean?!"

"It means that this is one of two times in the last fifteen years that I have ever seen this happen. I'm pleased to announce that this is a normal pregnancy. You can make an appointment to see your OB after this."

I burst into tears. I was probably just hormonal or something.

And from then on out, it WAS a normal pregnancy. For me, it was oddly normal. We didn't have to get a new test every other day! It was weird not having daily updates on my baby.

At the level-two ultrasound, we found out only two things: that this one was in fact a boy, and he was fat! He'd not only caught up, but the nurses were euphemistically calling him "healthy."

He got fatter, and so did I. I gained fifty pounds. About a month before I was due, the little boy got sick of the cramped quarters, and since there were no other ways for my body to expand, he made some room for himself—by dislocating six of my ribs.

That was the worst pain I have ever been in, and I have been hit by a car. The good news is, it only hurt when I breathed. So, I was thrilled when two weeks before my due date, my water broke in the middle of the night.

Mark drove me to Fairfax Hospital, dropped me off at the entrance to the women's center, and went to park the car, which was part of the plan. I was okay with that. But I was having contractions, my ribs still hurt, and my water seemed to be continuously breaking.

It was 4:00 a.m. Thanksgiving weekend. When I walked into the lobby, the only person anywhere in sight was the lady working at the front desk. I limped my way up to her and said, "I'm having a baby."

She was unimpressed. She looked me up in the system. Fortunately, since I'd been there before, it didn't take too long to fill out the paperwork, and then she gave me my little wristband and, without looking up at me, said, "Okay, there's the elevator. Take it up to the third floor!"

No wheelchair, no escort. I hobbled over to the elevator and took it to the third floor. And thank God the nurse was there waiting for me, because I just kind of fell into her arms.

She took me in and got me set up in a dry hospital gown on a hard, painful hospital bed and, yes, hooked up to a million monitors. The little boy already wanted to be just like his big sister, so he was breech, of course, which meant I had to have a C-section. I had to wait for the hospital to schedule it and get the room prepped.

A few hours later, the nurse wheeled me into the operating room. The anesthesiologist gave me a spinal tap, which was the first relief I had gotten from my ribs in several weeks. They lay me down, strapped my arms to the table, like Christ on the cross, and then they hung the curtain across my torso, I guess so I wouldn't be tempted to peek while they cut me open. Mark, in medical gown and cap, was escorted in, and we were all set to go!

Then the clock struck 7:00 a.m., and my delivery was put on hold while the nurses and anesthesiologist changed shifts. I was ready to go but had to wait for the staff to go first. They couldn't wait one minute. Or, as it turns out, seven. Our little boy, Finn, was born at 7:07 a.m. to a fresh-faced group of doctors and nurses. If I hadn't been so instantly in love with my little boy, I might've been kind of annoyed.

Even though he'd had a small, slow beginning, my little underachiever was overcompensating. Finn was two weeks early and nearly nine pounds!

Finn was my chubby, sweet, butterball baby. When Hope came to the hospital to meet him, she kept giggling at every funny face and noise he made. She laughed and called him "baby brother."

We got our two kids. It was not easy to bring them both into the world, and it hasn't been easy to take care of them and raise them and feed them and teach them. But since day one, it has been easy to love them, with all my heart.

Epilogue

My mom was an atheist who believed in ghosts. Well, really, just the one.

My grandparents, my mom's parents, were what we in NJ call Christmas Catholics. They went to church only on Christmas and Easter. And yet, they sent their kids, my mom included, to Catholic school, and this was back in the good old days of any transgression earning you a wrap on the knuckles by the nun in charge. By the time my mom had grown up, in the sixties, and met my dad, another fallen Catholic, they were close to ready to give up on the Church.

My parents had three kids together, and each of their kids' religious upbringing marks their religious descent. My brother, Brian, the oldest, got baptized, went to CCD (that's Catholic Sunday school), and received his Holy Communion (that's Catholic graduation). My sister, Heather, was also baptized and also went to CCD, but she never graduated. And then there was me, the last born. I did get baptized, but I never had to go to school on Sunday.

As a kid, I loved having Sundays free. But as I've gotten older, I have often wondered if I missed out after all. Whereas others know what happens when those they love die, I don't know. I don't know what to believe.

My mom's father passed away when my mom was in her early thirties. I was four years old, so I didn't know Grandpa well, but I know my mom loved him, that Grandpa was warm and generous to his beloved little girl. When he died, my parents had recently divorced and Mom was looking after three kids. I don't remember much about that time period, but I have two little kids now, and I can't imagine dealing with three, alone, especially while also grieving the loss of a parent.

I don't remember the funeral. I assume we weren't allowed to go. But I remember that time period. I remember my mom crying quietly to herself, sitting alone in a dark corner of the house and sobbing. I walked up to her and asked her what was wrong. She said, "I miss my dad." I don't think I even understood that he was Grandpa. I definitely didn't understand death. But I wrapped my little arms around my mom and hugged her. She stroked my back, and whether to console herself or because she really believed it, my mom said, "I know that my dad's up in Heaven, looking out for me."

I didn't know what to believe. I liked the thought that Grandpa was looking out for Mom. But as I grew up, I realized that if Grandpa was in Heaven looking out for my mom, he was doing a pretty awful job of it.

We were poor. I remember my mom crying over her checkbook while trying to pay utility bills. There was so much anxiety in the checkout line at the grocery store. What would we have to put back? My mom was plagued by bad relationships. She dated one guy who tortured and belittled us, her kids, but refused to marry her even though, for some reason, she wanted that. Then she dated a lawyer, a man who actually had money to offer but didn't want the kids she brought with her. Finally, she found a good one. A nice guy who loved her and loved us, until she got sick.

At thirty-nine, she had to have a mastectomy and radiation. She survived breast cancer, but her boyfriend left her, and us. He couldn't take watching her get sick. He wouldn't take care of her. Grandpa was there, though. He would make sure she was okay. At least, that's what she liked to say.

When she was forty-three, she suffered the first of four debilitating strokes. Each subsequent stroke stripped her of a few more of her abilities. She went from being able to read, write, do math, and hold down a job to not being able to read at all, handle numbers, or walk very well without falling over. Despite what must have been an incredible burden for her to bear, my mom was always warm and generous and held me close to her heart.

Eventually, we found the right doctor, and the strokes stopped. By that point, Mom had mostly stopped suggesting Grandpa was looking out for her. I'd already fully given up on him. Good thing too, because not long after her strokes stopped, Mom got diagnosed with terminal cancer.

Mom moved in with me and my new husband, who was less than happy about the arrangement. I spent a lot of time with my mom in those last few months of her life, but I could never bring myself to talk about how she felt about dying or anything that came too close to acknowledging that she was going to die. But Heather, my sister, who sometimes took Mom for the weekend and who spent a lot of time with us, Heather had no hang-ups about asking hard questions.

One day, Heather, Mom, and I were sitting together on my couch, and Heather said, "Mom, what do you think happens when you die?"

Mom said, "I don't know. I hope I go to Heaven. I hope I get to see my dad there."

Then we all started crying and hugging each other, and my mom kind of pushed us back so she could look us in the eye. And she said, "Listen, girls, I promise that if I do go to Heaven that I will look out for you."

I didn't know what to believe, but secretly I hoped that if

Mom did look out for us kids, that she would do a better job than Grandpa.

On her last night on Earth, we were at my sister's apartment. Mom was lying in the spare room. Brian and his dog were in the living room. Heather and I were lying on either side of Mom. She'd been mostly unconscious for hours. But Mom started struggling, moaning, fighting with some unseen demons.

Heather and I stroked her hair and spoke to her, saying, "Mom, you can let go now. We'll be okay. Your kids will be fine. Go to Heaven now. Go be with your dad." I don't know if Mom believed, in the end, but that seemed to soothe her, and she settled down into a deep sleep. Heather and I left her to sleep.

An hour or so later, we were all woken up by the dog, barking, three times. I ran to Mom's room. Heather called out, "Is she gone?" I didn't need to touch mom's body to know. I could see, just from looking at her, that some part of her had indeed gone.

Later that day, Brian, Heather, and I were sitting around talking. Brian said, "What about the dog, huh? I think he saw Mom's soul, flying up to Heaven."

And I didn't know what to believe, but I hope that that's true.

My life fell apart when my mom died. She was the person I was closest to in the world, the person who had loved me the most, and she was gone. About a year after she died, I was alone in the house I shared with my soon to be ex-husband, angry cleaning. I was sweeping with a vengeance, thinking about how mad I was at my husband for being so cold, how angry I was at myself for having married him, and how mad I was at the world for having taken my mom away from me. I needed her. I missed her. I was beginning to forget the sound of her voice, the way she smelled, how it felt to be held by her. And I needed that so much right then. I was about to break the broom in my effort to not break myself when suddenly I felt something. It was like someone wrapped a warm blanket over my shoulders, and I relaxed into the feeling. And then I heard, clear as if she was right beside me, my mom's voice. She just said "Jess."

Even though I didn't see her, I felt her. And I didn't know what to believe, but it felt as if my mom had crossed some barrier so that I could hear her voice once more, to let me know that she was still looking out for me.

That feeling stayed with me, buoyed me, over the next several rough years. Then I found Mark and we got married, and we had our baby girl, Hope. The love I feel for her goes beyond anything I could ever have imagined.

When she was about eight months old, Hope had these adorable little Shirley Temple curls. Everyone would look at my husband and me, with our straight hair, and wonder where she got them. I can tell you—they're from my mom. If you held up a picture of mom at eight months and one of my daughter, you'd see that they look like sisters.

Having my baby girl remind me of my mom was sort of a mixed blessing. This one night, I was alone with Hope, trying to get her to eat. Babies are cute, but they are not always great company. She was mostly refusing to eat and making a mess, and I was alone with my thoughts. I wished that my mom was there, because she'd know what to do. If there was one thing my mom loved more than her own children, it was babies. My mom was a professional baby whisperer. If there was a baby anywhere in a five-mile radius, my mom would find it and have that thing cooing and giggling in seconds. My mom started asking me to give her grandkids at an inappropriately young age. And yet, she died before any of us had our own babies.

Sitting there, alone with Hope, I was wishing that my mom was there so that she could help, but more because I wished she would've gotten to meet her grandbaby. And I wished that Hope could've gotten to meet her grandma.

And then Hope knocked the bowl of gruel on the floor and I left her for a minute to get a towel to clean up the mess. When I came back into the room, Hope was cooing and giggling. She was all alone in the room, but seemed to be communicating with someone, as if there was a professional baby whisperer close by. I said, "Mom?" She didn't answer me, but I felt her there.

I didn't know what to believe, but I felt as if Mom had crossed some barrier to meet her grandbaby, and maybe to let me know that Mom was going to look out for her too.

When Hope was four, she was a better conversationalist, though she asked a ton of questions. We were all at the dinner table one night, Hope, my husband Mark, me, and baby brother, and Hope was trying to figure everything out. She'd just been told, not for the first time, that Daddy and Mommy did not grow up together. To further illustrate the point, I said, "Mommy grew up with Aunt Heather and Uncle Brian. They are my brother and sister. Daddy grew up with Uncle Grant. That's his brother. And Grandma is Uncle Grant and Daddy's mom."

Hope's eyes grew wide and she asked, "But Mommy, where's your mommy?"

I hesitated at how to word it. Settled on, "She's gone, honey. She's no longer here."

"Oh." Then, very casually, "She's dead?"

"Yes." I got tears in my eyes. "My mommy's dead."

"Oh." Hope reached over, putting her little hand on my arm and stroking it. "It's okay, Mommy. Your mommy's in Heaven."

I don't always know what to believe, but I have Hope.

Acknowledgments

Normally, writing a book is somewhat of a solitary pursuit. In this case, it took a very large village.

I am a storyteller, and this book is a collection of stories, most of which I have performed in front of audiences. In the storytelling world, people say that storytelling is a two-way art. We, the storytellers, receive feedback from the audience and our stories change because of that. Considering, I feel I have to thank, first and foremost, the audiences. Thank you for coming to share in my stories, and for having made them better in the process.

I also need to thank every producer I've worked for. Whether you brought me in for a podcast, a TV show, a radio program, a festival, or a storytelling show at a library, museum, on a field, on zoom, or in a theater – you have given me reason to write, to craft, to improve my stories. Thank you for the work – and for the deadlines.

Thank you to my writing groups (past, present, and future), and my friends who keep me accountable – Joanne Lozar Glenn, Urmilla Khanna, Lisa Liebow, Mary Lucas, Jayne Raparelli, and Paula Tarnapol Whitacre.

A special thank you to my Better Said Than Done family. This includes everyone who has come to the shows, and the Women's Storytelling Festival, and all of the storytellers who I have had, and continue to have, the privilege of working with. And especially to the volunteers who have given so much to supporting the art of storytelling. There are too many people to list all, but particularly: Nick Baskerville, Judy Clapper, Stacy Crickmer, Alex Dixon, Bill Grella, Carol Moore, Miriam Nadel, Sarah Snyder, Cyndi Wish, and Andrea Young.

Thank you to the many storytellers who have given generously of their time to help me with "it all," especially Sara Armstrong, Sheila Arnold, Lona Bartlett, Norm Brecke, Jim Brulé, Alton Chung, Fanny Crawford, Laura Deal, Carmen Deedy, Megan DuBois, Meredith Eaton, Heather Forest, Susan Gordon, Rachel Hedman, Megan Hicks, Andrea Kamens, Erin Lovelien, Misty Mator, Jennifer Munro, Andy Offutt Irwin, Laura Packer, Karyn Page-Davies, Sam Pearsall, Anne Rutherford, Ellouise Schoettler, Regina Stoops, Mary Supley, Jude Treder-Wolff, and Joel Ying. And last, but certainly not least, the OG, Mr. Ed Stivender. I'll always take your notes. And thank you to the many other friends I have made in the storytelling world. When I found storytelling, and found fellow storytellers and storylovers, I finally found my people.

Thank you to the team at Tucker DS Press, specifically Scott Ryan and David Bushman.

To my beta readers - Lyn Ford, Bonnie Gardner, Claire Hennessy, Len Kruger, Jack Scheer – thank you for putting up with my many questions and thank you for being so willing to look at "just one more thing, and by tomorrow if you don't mind." Your insights surpassed my anxiety.

Love to my family, who were there, who are still here, and who have already moved on. Thank you to my sister, for having been there and here, the most. To my family members by marriage or choice—you may be relatively new, but you are loved just as much.

And here's to you, Mr. Robinson. I love you more than you will know.

About the Author

Jessica Robinson is the Founding Executive Director of Better Said Than Done, the Northern Virginia-based storytelling organization that, in addition to its semi-monthly shows, hosts the annual Women's Storytelling Festival. A spoken-word storyteller, Jessica has performed at Exchange Place at the International Storytelling Festival, on WGBH's "Stories from the Stage," and for the Stone Soup, the Washington Folk, the Florida, and the Hampton Storytelling festivals. Jessica is a 2023 ORACLE Award recipient from the National Storytelling Network.

In addition to magazines, reviews, and anthologies, Jessica is the author of Caged (under pen name JP Robinson) and co-author of the anthology *Roar: True Tales of Women Warriors*. By day, Jessica still runs the corporate video production company she started not long after graduating from film school. In her free time, she coaches soccer, chauffeurs children around, and plays one-sided fetch with her dog.

Jessica is a keynote speaker, workshop leader, and instructor. Find more at jessicapiscitellirobinson.com

JESSICA PISCITELLI ROBINSON

MORE BOOKS FROM FAYETTEVILLE MAFIA AND TUCKER DS PRESS

ORDER AT TUCKERDSPRESS.COM

www.ingramcontent.com/pod-product-compliance
Lightning Source LLC
Chambersburg PA
CBHW071149120626
46546CB00006B/2184